"Robyn Whitaker's lucid an[   ] reader to let the Bible be what it is rather than force it into preconceived categories and to keep in mind that the goal of interpretation is love. This engaging book should be read by any student embarking on the study of the Bible, especially those who come from a conservative background and are anxious about the effects of critical scholarship."

—JOHN J. COLLINS
Yale University

"Whitaker invites us to let the breath of God breathe when we read the Bible, speaking to us today not as propositional one-liners but as an unfolding story of God's love for humanity. Whitaker deftly shows us the ways in which this hermeneutic of love is modeled for us throughout Scripture and gives us key insights on how to interpret the Bible today. This book is a critically important resource for any Christian who wants to encounter God's love as it is unfolding in history in our present moment."

—MEGHAN HENNING
University of Dayton

"This unique book integrates Whitaker's impressive academic expertise with everyday matters of faith and applies both to reading the Bible and to discerning how God continues to speak to God's people through this living, dynamic sacred text. Whitaker explores what we can learn about how to interpret the Bible from the Bible itself with the premise that anyone can quote the Bible—even the devil—but that doesn't mean one is correct. In a world keen on proof-texting and my-way-or-the-highway, Whitaker challenges the ways the Bible is used to condemn and exclude and advocates replacing such use with a hermeneutic of love, inviting readers deeper into conversation with God and following the example of Jesus. This book is a gift and excellent resource for the academy, the church, and, in Whitaker's words, 'those hovering around her edges.'"

—JENN STRAWBRIDGE
University of Oxford

"*Approachable, engaging, honest,* and *thoughtful* are words I would use to recommend Robyn J. Whitaker's *Even the Devil Quotes Scripture* to Christians wanting to know more about biblical interpretation. Drawing upon her own experiences, Whitaker invites readers to think about some of the Bible's most puzzling pieces, such as contradicting stories and multiple versions of the same story. Throughout the book Whitaker models what she describes as a hermeneutic of love, a way of reading the Bible that privileges listening to others, doing no harm, and embracing compassion. This book will be an excellent resource for anyone teaching the Bible in congregational or seminary settings."

—LYNN HUBER
Elon University

Even the Devil Quotes Scripture

Reading the Bible on Its Own Terms

Robyn J. Whitaker

WILLIAM B. EERDMANS PUBLISHING COMPANY
GRAND RAPIDS, MICHIGAN

Wm. B. Eerdmans Publishing Co.
4035 Park East Court SE, Grand Rapids, Michigan 49546
www.eerdmans.com

29 28 27 26 25 24 23   1 2 3 4 5 6 7

ISBN 978-0-8028-8203-5

Library of Congress Cataloging-in-Publication Data

A catalog record for this book is available from the Library
of Congress.

For my parents, Peter and Gillian,
who first taught me to love the Bible

Contents

Acknowledgments

In many ways I have been preparing to write this book for about twenty-five years. I entered seminary as a twenty-year-old, conservative Christian, determined to read the Bible literally and not let any of those "liberal" scholars upset my conservative evangelical faith. Kicking and screaming, I found my faith rapidly deconstructed as I entered the world of academic theological study and discovered that my fundamentalist view of Scripture was not sustainable in the face of both historical evidence and where God was leading me.

I am enormously grateful for the education I received from those who taught me at the United Faculty of Theology in Melbourne, but the deconstruction was more masterfully done than the reconstruction. It has felt like a longer and far lonelier process to rebuild a faith that can embrace the rigor of academic insights but retains an evangelical heart that recognizes the way the Holy Spirit continues to speak to God's people through the Bible.

In many ways my students have helped me do this work. I did my PhD at the University of Chicago Divinity School, a brilliant place to have been formed as a scholar. But it was the questions from students I taught at Union Seminary in New York and within the University of Divinity, Melbourne, that forced me to integrate that lofty academic learning with everyday matters of faith. These students demanded to bring their whole selves to the text (as they should), and they wanted to know how it spoke to pressing contemporary questions, such as the Black Lives Matter movement, which was in its infancy when I was at Union, or national debates about same-gender marriage more recently in Australia. They want to know how to interpret the Bible for their diverse communities with their diverse experiences and contexts. They do not settle for interpretation that hides in historical obscurities or attempts so-called objective historical-critical readings. These students have pushed and challenged me as I have them, and I know that I am a better teacher for it.

One does not write a book alone. In addition to the work of wonderful scholars whose research has challenged, stimulated, and taught me a great deal, there is an equally wonderful community of colleagues and friends who have read drafts of this book and offered feedback. My thanks go to Daniel Nellor, who posed brilliant and challenging questions to the drafts he read, and to my colleagues William Loader, Geoff Thompson, and Glen O'Brien, who shared their scholarly expertise and engaged in helpful conversations along the way. Trevor Thompson, my editor at Eerdmans, has been a great encouragement since I first pitched the project. I am grateful for his guidance and suggestions for the manuscript. Thanks also to Adrian Jackson, Peter Byrnes, Kylie Crabbe, Peter Whitaker, Gillian Whitaker, and Katecia Taylor, who read drafts and gave feedback, and Kate Boyer and Esther Hamori for brainstorming titles.

I am grateful to Pilgrim Theological College and the Uniting Church in Australia, who granted me six months sabbatical to help complete this book. Research leave is such a gift for the creative space it affords, and I hope that, in return, this book might be a gift and resource for the church and those hovering around her edges.

Lastly, I give my thanks to my husband, Peter, for his abiding support of my vocation, for his reminders to stop procrastinating, for the glasses of wine at the end of the day, and for being the best lockdown buddy one could imagine. Much of this book was written during Melbourne's record-breaking Covid lockdown. It would have been immeasurably harder without his good humor and company. Agador Spartacus and Hudson, our two boisterous retrievers, also provided enthusiastic affection and constant companionship in my home office. Unlike many of us, they lived their best lives during lockdown.

This book is dedicated to my parents, Peter and Gillian. They were the first people to teach me to read, interpret, and love the Bible. I will forever be grateful for their influence and for their Christian faith, which has shaped my own.

Introduction

When you stop trying to force the Bible to be something it's not . . . then you are free to revel in what it is: living, breathing, confounding, surprising.

— RACHEL HELD EVANS
Inspired

As a teenager I was delighted to receive one of those hefty leather-clad, zip-up, NIV Bibles that weighed a ton and had all the words of Jesus in red ink. All the pious Christian youth had them and I wanted to be like them, signaling to others how serious I was about my faith. This particular one was navy blue and a birthday gift from my parents. On the inside cover, my father, a clergyman, wrote, "May you have the wisdom to discern the kernel from the chaff."*

The idea that some parts of the Bible are "kernel" and some parts can be set aside like "chaff" was challenging to me at the time. It's the Bible. It's all true! Can any of it be considered chaff? For years I read the Bible with a sincere and fervent desire to embrace all of it; to take it literally as a guide to life. I would have told you that I considered it all equally important and equally true, and I thought that defending this was the best way to show my commitment to God.

I now no longer read the Bible literally, but this does not mean I do not take it seriously. The reality is I never really treated the whole Bible equally even when I thought I did. My NIV

---

* In hindsight, this is a very Wesleyan formulation, which is not surprising given my father trained as a Methodist minister. Wesley wrote that "every truth which is revealed in the oracles of God is undoubtedly of great importance. Yet it may be allowed that some of those which are revealed therein are of greater importance than others, as being more immediately conducive to the grand end of all [salvation]." John Wesley, *Sermons on Several Occasions* (London: Wesleyan Conference Office, 1872), sermon 73.

Bible had red letters for the bits that Jesus said, and most of the underlined and highlighted passages were from the New Testament, not the Old Testament. Bits of Genesis and some of Isaiah were underlined and memorized so that I too could quote the passages that "proved" creation or that Jesus was the prophesied Messiah, but large parts in between were not touched—a sign of where I spent most of my devotional time.

In truth, we all read in a way that privileges some parts of the Bible and gives little attention to others. We have favorite passages, canons within the canon, parts that we read often, and parts that we skip over either because we don't particularly connect with them, we can't make sense of them, or the portrait of God they offer challenges our beliefs or unsettles our faith.

I have learned that it is impossible to read the Bible in a literalistic way, and I now believe we are not meant to. We are meant to take the Bible seriously, not literally. I have come to appreciate the harder parts of the Bible, the bits that are strange, unsettling, or impossible to fathom. I appreciate that the deeper questions they provoke draw us in and prompt curiosity. I appreciate that the difficult parts keep us humble as interpreters. They also require us to go back to the starting point and examine our assumptions. What is the Bible? What do we expect from it? And, how do we best read and interpret it? That is what this book is about.

The Approach of This Book

Because I am a biblical scholar and because those formative years spent within evangelical Christianity taught me to value the Bible so highly, the Bible itself is always the starting point for me.* I do not begin here with doctrine or denominational claims,

---

* This is the classic Protestant approach to the Bible. Sixteenth-century Protestants wrote about *sola scriptura sui ipsius interpres* (Scripture alone as it interprets itself) as that which governs both faith and doctrine.

although both shape me. The key question of this book is this: What can we learn about interpreting the Bible from the Bible itself? Are there clues on those ancient and precious pages that tell us what the Bible is and how we best engage it?

Anyone can quote the Bible, but that does not mean they know it, understand it, or have interpreted it well. After all, even the devil quotes Scripture. Matthew and Luke's Gospels record how Jesus was tested by the devil for forty days prior to beginning his ministry (Matt. 4:1–11; Luke 4:1–12). One of the ways the devil tries to persuade Jesus to test God and prove himself is by quoting Psalm 91. Jesus quotes the Bible back. Quoting the Bible to make a point is a form of interpretation. It does not mean the one quoting is correct. Over the centuries, the Bible has been quoted and used to justify things that are at odds with its central message. In early 2022, for example, as Russian military forces invaded Ukraine, Russian President Vladimir Putin quoted the Bible at a rally—"there is no greater love than giving up one's soul (life) for one's friends" (a paraphrase of John 15:13). In its biblical context, this verse is something Jesus says to his disciples after telling them there is no greater commandment than to love one another. Jesus says this on his way to the cross, not to war. In the same week that Putin cited a Bible verse to justify his war, leaders in the USA were calling him a war criminal for deliberately targeting civilians. Being able to quote the Bible does not guarantee that one has heard its message or attempts to live out its overarching ethic. So how then do we read and interpret the Bible in ways that are faithful to the gospel? What are the guiding ethical principles?

What I suggest is that when we read the Bible on its own terms, we discover that clues to interpretation abound. The Bible itself testifies to how it was read by ancient priests, prophets, scribes, Jesus, Paul, and others whose words were later declared sacred by the church. When we start with the Bible itself, we see how biblical writers themselves used and interpreted their own sacred texts. The Bible is full of such examples within its own pages. We will look at how Ezra and Nehemiah (re)interpret the Law of Moses after the exile, and we will sit with Jesus as he interprets the same law centuries later. We will unpack the various strategies biblical authors use to interpret earlier traditions and touch briefly on the ways biblical interpretation has changed throughout the centuries. The surprise, for some, is that inner-biblical interpretation is flexible, adaptable, and highly contextual, indicating a dynamic, living tradition.

Lastly, I will propose a hermeneutic, an interpretive lens, for interpreting the Bible based on the Bible itself. I call this a hermeneutic of love.

A Lesson from Jacob

One of my favorite Bible stories is the one where Jacob wrestles God in the night (Gen. 32:22–32). It is a strange, moving, and, frankly, hilarious story. It is also a wonderful metaphor for faith and biblical interpretation.

The story goes that on the cusp of a potentially dangerous reunion with his brother Esau, Jacob finds himself alone as evening falls. "A man" mysteriously appears and wrestles with Jacob. We are not told why. Now Jacob is stubborn, and he refuses to let go of the man, demanding a blessing from this wrestling stranger before he will release him. As the dawn breaks, the man says to Jacob, "you have striven with God," and gives him the blessing he has demanded. Jacob realizes he has been wrestling with God the whole time and is astonished to find he has survived!

The Hebrew term we translate as "wrestle" literally means to "get dusty." Jacob spent the night getting dusty with God and leaves with a limp, a new name, and a blessing. When we wrestle with Scripture in the way Jacob wrestled with God, we cannot but walk away changed. Sometimes we walk away with what feels like a wound, challenged and confronted by our own failings and the need to change or disturbed by the call of God to bring justice and peace to the world. Sometimes the wrestling leads to blessing, the kind of blessing that is exactly what we need—comfort, affirmation, and the knowledge we are God's children. And if we wrestle long enough, we might emerge, like Jacob, with a new identity. It takes time to develop and grow into new identities. Jacob's was forged through many hours of engaging with the divine through the darkest of nights. We too need to spend hours with this sacred text to really discover all the challenges and blessings therein. We need to sit with it even when it feels like the dawn will never come. When we do, we find ourselves in its story, we learn the history of our people, we recognize our struggles in theirs as well as our calling, and in doing so we emerge with a new sense of ourselves, a new identity as one of God's beloved and chosen people.

There is an enormous intimacy in wrestling. You have to be physically close to the other person and incredibly vulnerable, trusting that while the other may win, you won't be permanently harmed. You also can't wrestle with one foot in and the other out! In wrestling with Scripture, we must bring our whole selves into dialogue with the other. Bringing our whole selves into conversation with the Bible means bringing our beliefs, fears, prejudices, loves, passions, experiences, and knowledge. Some of these will emerge transformed.

If you are willing to do a little wrestling, then keep reading. But be warned: to benefit most from this book, you don't just need to be willing to wrestle with my views or even the Bible's, but also with your own. We all come to this text with a set of preconceived ideas and beliefs. When we seek to read the Bible on its own terms, we might find those challenged. We might get a bit dusty.

What Is the Bible?

The Bible is a witness to the living reality that (is) God.

—GEOFF THOMPSON
"Metaphors for Scripture"

Scripture . . . is the air we breathe, the water we Christian
fish swim in.

—DALE MARTIN
Biblical Truths

Being wholly and verbally God-given, Scripture is without error or fault in all its teaching, no less in what it
states about God's acts in creation, about the events of
world history, and about its own literary origins under God,
than in its witness to God's saving grace.

— CHICAGO STATEMENT ON BIBLICAL INERRANCY

In this chapter we will lay out some basics, beginning with what the Bible is and is not. We could also call this next section "things I learned in seminary that rocked my world and I wish someone had told me sooner."

What Is the Bible?

"The Bible says . . ." is a common phrase. Used to appeal to the Bible as an authority on any range of contemporary issues—sexuality, marriage, gender, abortion, voluntary assisted dying, or climate change—such a statement assumes the Bible is a definitive entity as well as one that speaks with a singular voice on complex issues. We will get to the second part of this later as we grapple with the tension between the unity and diversity of the Bible, but for now we need to clarify what we mean by "the Bible." What is the Bible?

We can answer the question of what the Bible is in at least two ways. The first approach is historical, literary, and scholarly. It asks questions like, What is this ancient collection of texts we call "the Bible"? What do we know about the communities who wrote and preserved them? What genres, themes, and types of writing do we find in the Bible? What does it tell us about the ancient world and the way a particular group of people thought about God, life, justice, or suffering? These kinds of questions do not rely on faith, although they can enrich faith, and can be asked by any curious person, historian, or scholar.

The second approach relates to faith and is of particular interest to those exploring faith, grappling with faith, or living within the Christian community: Why do Christians consider this particular collection of religious texts sacred, unique, or holy? Why is this the text we read in church, usually to the exclusion of all others? Is it authoritative, and in what way? And what does that mean for how we read it?

A Historical View

The answer to "what is the Bible?" depends upon your tradition. The Christian Bible can vary quite a lot. "Different communities have different Bibles," write Amy-Jill Levine and Marc Brettler about the Bibles of Jews and Christians around the globe.* The Protestant Bible has sixty-six books, and the Catholic Bible has a few extra because the Catholic Church (and some Anglicans and Orthodox Christians) consider the Apocrypha to be inspired by God as well.† The table on page 11 shows some of these differences.

Historically, the Bible of Jesus and his disciples would have been some version of what we commonly call the Old Testament. It is unlikely that the canon of Jewish scriptures were fixed until about the second century CE, so we don't know exactly what Jesus heard read in synagogue except that it would have included the Torah (Pentateuch), Psalms, and some prophets. However, when Paul and other New Testament writers quote from "the Scriptures" in the New Testament, they quote the Greek translation of the Hebrew Bible called the Septuagint (LXX for short). The Septuagint differs from the Hebrew Bible, both in terms of hav-

---

* Amy-Jill Levine and Marc Zvi Brettler, *The Bible With and Without Jesus: How Jews and Christians Read the Same Stories Differently* (New York: HarperCollins, 2020), 3.

† The Apocrypha (literally meaning "hidden things") is a collection of Jewish texts from the intertestamental period, the period between the Old Testament and New Testament, and includes things like the stories of the Maccabees, Judith, Tobit, and extra sections to Daniel.

ing extra books and sometimes having different or extra chapters within certain books. So the "Bible" of the earliest Christians is a difficult thing to name precisely. Depending on one's language, location, or even just what scrolls your local synagogue had, the "Bible" one heard read in the first century CE would have differed.*

The term "Bible" is based on a Greek word meaning "book." The Christian Bible, however, is not one book but rather a collection of texts written over roughly one thousand years by many different authors writing in three different languages (Hebrew, Greek, and a little Aramaic). These texts are arranged into the thirty-nine (or more) books of the Old Testament, written between approximately 1000 and 200 BCE, and the twenty-seven books of the New Testament, written between about 50 and 120 CE in response to the life, death, and resurrection of Jesus.

The New Testament denotes the section of the Bible that is about Jesus. It is still deeply Jewish and was written by Jews, but by Jews who had come to believe that Jesus was the Messiah. All of the twenty-seven writings in the New Testament were written in Greek, and all attempt to draw out the significance of Jesus's life, death, and resurrection for their communities. They did so by writing letters, writing narratives about Jesus's life, or using other biblical genres to reveal a theological truth.

While there is a lot of diversity, in broad and practical terms we can say that the Christian Bible is a small library of varying size: a collection of ancient texts from the Jewish and Christian traditions that speak about those communities' experiences of God and the world. However, depending upon what kind of Bible one picks up— Protestant, Catholic, or Orthodox—the contents page will look rather different.

* By "Bible" here I mean the physical collection of sacred texts. Early Christians certainly already had a sense of Scripture, of holy writings, that included Torah (Pentateuch), prophets, Psalms, and other writings but with less clearly defined parameters.

TABLE I: COMPARISON OF BIBLES

	Roman Catholic	*Protestant*	*Orthodox Bibles*	*Jewish Bible*
Old Testament Books	46	39	Approx. 51–53	24*
Translation Based On	Latin (Vulgate) from Greek (LXX) plus Hebrew	Hebrew (and a little Aramaic)	Greek (LXX)	Hebrew (and a little Aramaic)
Books (Italics denote those books not found in the Protestant Bible)	**Pentateuch (Law)** Gen. Exod. Lev. Num. Deut.	**Pentateuch (Law)** Gen. Exod. Lev. Num. Deut.	**Pentateuch (Law)** Gen. Exod. Lev. Num. Deut.	**Pentateuch (Law)** Gen. Exod. Lev. Num. Deut.
	Historical Books Josh. Judg. Ruth 1 & 2 Sam. 1 & 2 Kings 1 & 2 Chron. Ezra Neh. *Esther (longer)* *1 & 2 Maccabees*	**Historical Books** Josh. Judg. Ruth 1 & 2 Sam. 1 & 2 Kings 1 & 2 Chron. Ezra Neh. Esther	**Historical Books** Josh. Judg. Ruth 1 & 2 Sam. 1 & 2 Kings 1 & 2 Chron. Ezra Neh. *Esther (longer)*	**Nevi'im** <u>Former Prophets</u> Josh. Judg. Sam. Kings <u>Latter Prophets</u> Isa. Jer.

* This number is lower than the Protestant Old Testament, which is based on the Jewish Bible, because the Jewish Bible has books like Samuel, Kings, and Chronicles as one book each (versus 1 and 2 Samuel or 1 and 2 Kings in Christian versions) and clusters the twelve minor prophets into one "Book of Twelve." Note, too, the difference in arrangement in the Hebrew Bible compared with the Old Testament of Christians.

Roman Catholic	Protestant	Orthodox Bibles	Jewish Bible
Wisdom	**Wisdom**	*Jud.*	Ezek.
Job	Job	*Tob.*	Twelve
Ps. (150)	Ps. (150)	*1 & 2 Macc.*	Prophets
Prov.	Prov.	*3 & 4 Macc.*	(Hos., Joel,
Eccles.	Eccles.		Amos, Obad.,
(Qoheleth)	(Qoheleth)	**Poetic Books**	Jonah, Mic.,
Song of Songs	Song of	Ps. (*151*)	Nah., Hab.,
Wisd. of Sol.	Songs	*Odes*	Zeph., Hag.,
Sirach		Prov.	Zech., Mal.)
	Prophets	Eccles.	
Prophets	Isa.	(Qoheleth)	**Ketuvim**
Isa.	Jer.	Song of	**(Writings)**
Jer.	Lam.	Songs	Ps. (150)
Lam.	Ezek.	Job	Prov.
Bar.	Dan.	*Wisd. of Sol.*	Job
Ezek.	(12 chaps.)	*Sir.*	Song of Songs
Dan.	Hos.	*Pss. of Sol.*	Ruth
(14 chaps.)	Joel		Lam.
Hos.	Amos	**Prophets**	Eccles.
Joel	Obad.	Hos.	(Qoheleth)
Amos	Jonah	Joel	Esther
Obad.	Mic.	Amos	Dan.
Jonah	Nah.	Obad.	Ezra-Neh.
Mic.	Hab.	Jonah	Chron.
Nah.	Zeph.	Mic.	
Hab.	Hag.	Nah.	
Zeph.	Zech.	Hab.	
Hag.	Mal.	Zeph.	
Zech.		Hag.	
Mal.		Zech.	
		Mal.	
		Isa.	
		Jer.	
		Bar.	
		Lam.	
		Letter of Jer.	
		Ezek.	

	Roman Catholic	Protestant	Orthodox Bibles	Jewish Bible
			Dan. (14 chaps., including Susanna, Bel and the Dragon)	
New Testament	27	27	27	—
Translation Based On	Greek	Greek	Greek	n/a

Manuscripts

We do not have *the* original Bible—there is no such thing. The modern Bible you have in your home or church is a carefully edited compilation based on over 5,700 ancient Greek manuscripts. If you count ancient manuscripts translated into Latin, Coptic, Syriac, and other languages, this number moves into the tens of thousands. These copies exist as thousands of ancient manuscripts and papyri ranging from tiny, inch-long scraps of text that have been ravaged by time to more complete versions of books and even collections of books. The oldest of these manuscripts dates to the second century CE, at least a hundred years after Jesus, meaning we will likely never recover any of the actual letters written by Paul or the first version of one of the gospels.* We have copies of copies of copies of the Bible's various texts that have been written out by hand, copied by hand, and translated by communities over hundreds of years.

There is a great deal of agreement in these early manuscripts, but there are also differences where a word has been changed

---

* The earliest existing manuscript of Mark's Gospel, P[45], dates to the early third century CE.

or a text is longer or shorter. Teams of scholarly editors have to make difficult decisions about which version is likely to be the earliest or more authentic, and that is normally the basis for the translation you read in your Bible. Usually, we readers cannot detect these editorial decisions in our English translations. If you have a study Bible, sometimes a variation is put in a footnote. And sometimes we can see places where a verse had been omitted based on evidence that it was not in the earliest manuscripts and was added later. For example, most modern Bibles are missing Matthew 17:21 and Mark 7:16, and those verse numbers are just skipped.*

Sometimes, however, editors leave in the ancient diversity. If you take a look at Mark 16 in your Bible, you will most likely see that the main story seems to stop at 16:8 with the line that the women "said nothing to anyone, for they were afraid." It is hardly a triumphant ending for a gospel, which is probably why some ancient manuscripts have one of two different endings, one that records the women did as commanded and Jesus appeared to them all (16:8b), and another that goes into a much longer account of the appearances and miracles that followed the resurrection (16:9–20). Most modern translations of the Bible include both these alternate endings under the subheadings "shorter ending" and "longer ending." While the shorter version, which ends at 16:8, is considered the oldest and most authentic, there is enough variation in the old manuscripts that the translators of modern Bibles have left in the alternatives for us to see.

---

* There are about sixteen examples of omitted verses in the New Testament. These are examples of instances where scribes have clearly added a sentence that was not in the earliest copies. As we have recovered more ancient manuscripts, we can see more clearly where such additions occur and hence remove them.

Translation Matters

As we consider what the Bible is, we also need to consider the nature of translation. Unless you fluently read ancient Hebrew and Greek, you are reading a translation. All translation is an act of interpretation, as decisions are made about which English word best reflects a Greek or Hebrew term out of the range of possibilities.

These days, English-speaking Christians have a plethora of Bibles to choose from, reflecting a range of translations. Some of these aim to be as literal as possible in translating the Greek or Hebrew text, others have explicit theological aims, and most make some concessions for English readability. Many times the exact translation we read does not matter too much. After all, the message of Scripture is in the whole, not each individual word or even phrase. But sometimes translations do make a huge difference. Consider for example the difference between these two translations of Galatians 2:16:

> We know that a person is justified not by the works of the law but through faith <u>in</u> Jesus Christ . . . (NRSV)

> Knowing that a man is not justified by the works of the law, but by the faith <u>of</u> Jesus Christ . . . (KJV)

The theological difference between justification (being made right with God) because of your faith "in" Christ and being justified because "of" Christ's own faithfulness to God cannot be overstated. One places the onus for salvation on the individual's belief and the other on the action of Jesus for humanity. The Greek of Galatians 2:16 is ambiguous and grammatically allows for either translation, so this is one of those cases where other factors influence translation, including what one thinks Paul is doing theologically and rhetorically in this letter. The translator's own theology comes into play, as no translator is entirely objective. Tomes have been written about this issue, and the majority of contemporary versions (NIV, ESV, NRSV) now translate it as faith *in* Christ, whereas the King James retains the old idea of the faith *of* Christ. I am personally partial to the King James Version in this case.

A second example of a translation issue occurs when ambiguity is introduced in the English. John 3:16 is a well-known verse, usually rendered in English as "for God so loved the world." Unfortunately, this translation conveys something the Greek does not. Most Christians interpret this famous phrase as a comment about the extent of God's love; that is, that God loved the world so very, very much. But the Greek here uses a word that points to the manner of God's love, and it would be better translated as "for in this way God loved the world, that he gave his only Son." *So* in English can have both senses, and the ambiguity that the translation introduces is not helpful. In John 3:16 the author is at pains to show that the nature of God's love can be seen most vividly in the death of Jesus on the cross—a self-giving and self-sacrificing kind of love. It is a comment about the nature of God's self-giving love in giving over his Son. That God loves the world a lot is a given.

A third kind of translation issue occurs with words that appear only once in the Bible (called *hapax legomena*). There are well over a thousand instances of these in the Bible. Often translators can work out the meaning of the Greek or Hebrew on the basis of similar words with similar roots or comparison with other ancient texts. In hundreds of cases, however, we have only the context to guess the meaning as there are no other existing instances of the word. A simple example is Genesis 6:14, "make yourself an ark of gopher wood." *Gopher* is a Hebrew term that only occurs in the Bible here, and we don't know what it means. In this case, the precise translation doesn't really matter, as it is describing the type of tree (literally "tree of g-ph-r").* But on other occasions more is at stake.

---

* Some modern translations have chosen "cypress" in its place, as that is a historically plausible wood for the time and place.

One example of this is the word *arsēnokoites*. Technically, it is not a hapax legomena, as it occurs twice in the New Testament (1 Cor. 6:9 and 1 Tim. 1:10), but it is a word whose meaning is highly contested, with significant ramifications. *Arsēnokoites* is a compound form of two Greek words: male (*arsēn*) and bed (*koites*). Paul possibly made it up. This has led some to suggest the word indicates men bedding other men or men who are bedded. But knowing the two parts of the word doesn't necessarily help. We have lots of compound words in English that mean something quite different from the two words from which they are made. Consider, for example, *butterfly*, *peacock*, or *rainbow*, where knowing the individual words would not necessarily help one come to the right conclusion. *Arsēnokoites* appears in a list of vices so it is a behavior that Paul thinks is inappropriate for Christians, but what kind of behavior is it? There is no space here to summarize all of the complex arguments regarding translation options. What is pertinent is getting a sense of what is at stake. A survey of the various English Bible translations of *arsēnokoites* offers up a range of terms, including "homosexuals," "pederasts" (an adult male who sleeps with young men or boys), "sodomites," "practicing homosexuals," "male prostitutes," or "abusers of themselves" with men.* These are vastly different things, ranging from same-sex attraction to selling one's body (or being enslaved as a prostitute) to the rape of young males. Depending on the translation, one can come to very different conclusions about what precisely is being condemned here, with significant implications for the modern world.

Another type of translation issue occurs where the translated word can convey something the original may not have meant. In Exodus 34:29–35 Moses is described as coming down Mount Sinai with a shining face after receiving the Ten Commandments

* See Dale Martin, "*Arsenokoitēs* and *Malakos*: Meanings and Consequences," in *Biblical Ethics and Homosexuality*, ed. Robert L. Brawley (Louisville: Westminster John Knox, 1996), 117–36.

and communing with God. In the original Hebrew, the word for horns (*qeren*) is used to describe the rays of light coming out of his face—literally "horns of light." Ancient Jewish commentators understood this as a figurative reference to light as did the translators of the Septuagint, who rather than using the Greek word for horns chose to translate it as "his face was charged with glory" (*doxazō*). But in his fourth-century Latin translation of the Bible (the Vulgate), Jerome famously went with a literal translation, writing that Moses's "face was horned." This translation dominated medieval Christianity, leading Michelangelo and numerous other artists and iconographers to depict Moses with small horns sprouting from the top of his head. Why does this mistranslation matter?

Moses's "horns" were interpreted by later Christians as a sign that Jews were evil. While ancient deities were sometimes depicted with horns, suggesting they could symbolically represent divinity (which makes sense in the original story due to Moses's closeness to God), in the Christian tradition horns became associated with the devil. The evil beasts of Revelation 13, for example, have multiple horns. Such associations led to depictions of the devil as a man-beast with horns and, eventually, a tail. By the Middle Ages, Christians talked about Jews as children of the devil and some assumed that all Jews had horns. Moses and his kin were, literally, demonized. While the entire history of anti-Semitism cannot be attributed to one mistranslation, it has certainly not helped. Translation matters deeply.

Summary

Examining the Bible through the scholarly lens of history indicates it has a more complex background than we are often led to believe. In addition to the various number of books and the different translations that make up modern Bibles, the Bible also includes texts that range widely in terms of genre. The sixty-six "books" of the Bible are actually made up of letters, historical narratives, stories, biographies of Jesus, mythical tales, songs, prophetic utterances, poetry, and apocalypses. The implications are that we read different genres differently and a lot of the time our brains do this instinctively. We will look at how genre matters in later chapters as we interpret different texts.

Despite all this diversity and complexity, there is a common thread in that all these texts speak about humans' experiences of the divine. And not of just any deity, but a specific deity. A personal deity. A deity called YHWH (Yahweh), whose identity and name was revealed to the earliest Hebrews according to the stories in Genesis. And so the Bible tells the story of a family who becomes a tribal group and then a nation, who have a specific experience of God and enter into a covenantal relationship with that God. Everything else unfolds from there.

EXCURSUS:

OLD AND NEW TESTAMENTS—A NOTE ABOUT TERMS

Christians in the contemporary era are probably most familiar with the terms *Old Testament* and *New Testament* to label the two main sections of the Bible. These terms are not unproblematic and bear the historical weight of anti-Semitic sentiment and supersessionism. Something "old" can be inferred to be defunct or superseded by the "new," and some Christians have claimed exactly that when it comes to the Bible. The new is often privileged in modern Christian tradition.

Since the 1970s, some scholars have used the terms *Hebrew Bible*, *Jewish Bible*, or *First Testament* to refer to the Old Testament in the hope that this would counteract the idea that the "Old" Testament was defunct, inferior to, or lesser than the New Testament.* The Hebrew Bible is just that: a

---

* These labels were motivated by the best of interfaith intentions but are not without their problems and critics. See Amy-Jill Levine, *The*

collection of texts written in Hebrew (with a little Aramaic) made up of Law (Torah), Prophets (Navi'im), and Writings (Ketuvim). Most Jews refer to their Bible as Tanakh, an acronym for Torah, Navi'im, Ketuvim. The Old Testament that many Christians read starts in the same way, but what follows differs in both arrangement and in that it has a different number of books (see the table above). Moreover, some parts of the Christian church, such as Greek Orthodox Christians, use the Greek version of the Hebrew Bible, the Septuagint (LXX), as the basis for parts of the Old Testament, which is again quite different. To refer to modern Christian translations of the Septuagint as the "Hebrew Bible" is a misnomer.

I prefer to the use the language of *Older* and *Newer Testaments* to denote the two parts of the Christian Bible. It may seem a subtle change and is in no way perfect, but *older* and *newer* imply a relationship: these two parts of the Bible belong together in the Christian tradition and one does not make sense without the other. For ease of reading, however, I will use the traditional terms *Old Testament* and *New Testament* here.

Bible as Scripture: Inspired, Inerrant, Infallible?

We have outlined what the Bible is from a historical point of view, including highlighting the range of translation and manuscript traditions to show that "the Bible" as a single entity is actually a more complex and diverse thing than many of us have been taught. When I learned all this in my first year of seminary, I confess that it shook my then-conservative evangelical faith. There were times I

Misunderstood Jew: The Church and the Scandal of the Jewish Jesus (San Francisco: Harper, 2006), 193–96.

thought I must be crazy to believe in Jesus if so much of the Bible was so human and potentially imperfect. If it was imperfect and human, could it be trusted? And if the Bible couldn't be trusted, then was my whole faith based on something futile? It was like someone had pulled the bottom piece out of a tall Jenga tower and the whole thing was wobbling and on the point of collapse. I was forced to confront my own assumptions about why I believed the Bible and on what grounds it could be considered authoritative.

We turn now to matters of faith. To believe the words of the Bible in such a way that you become a follower of Jesus and shape your life around its message is an act of faith rather than something provable by science or even history. That does not make it lesser. Just different.

Christians have used a variety of words over the past two thousand years to describe the authority of the Bible. Some of them appear in the quotes with which I began this chapter—*inerrant, inspired, unique, infallible, holy, sacred, authoritative, transformative, witness,* or *testimony*—quotes designed to show the breadth of Christian articulation when it comes to the Bible. So let's examine the three main claims Christians use to refer to the nature of the Bible from a faith perspective—inspired, infallible, inerrant. We begin with inspiration.

Inspired

Ancient icons depict gospel writers like Mark with a quill in hand and an angel whispering words in his ear. Such images convey the belief that these Bible writers took dictation, every word being from God, with humans acting as a conduit for the divine and nothing more. Some people talk about inspiration in this way, suggesting "inspired" means words that were dictated by God. While the simplicity of this view is appealing, there are several problems with it, not least that the Bible itself is honest about the levels of human involvement.

One of the Bible verses I memorized in my youth was 2 Timothy 3:16: "All scripture is inspired by God." This verse was usually quoted as evidence that we could believe the Bible and trust it comes straight from God because it was "inspired." The Greek word often translated "inspired" in 2 Timothy 3:16 is an adjective that literally means God-breathed or God-spirited (*theopneustos*). It is the only time it is used in the Bible and so we don't have other passages to compare to help nuance the meaning, but the idea of God breathing out or dictating Scripture probably comes from here. We might think of it as being similar to the way God breathed into Adam and animated the earth creature God had molded (Gen. 2:7) or the way the Spirit comes upon or stirs up prophets and kings (1 Sam. 19:20; Rev. 1:10). The Greek word for spirit (*pneuma*) is based on the Hebrew term *ruakh*, which can mean breath, wind, or spirit. It can be ambiguous, but denotes the various ways the divine acts with human beings. Jesus himself referred to King David as speaking "by the Holy Spirit" when he composed what we know as Psalm 110, which is also a way of saying "inspired" by God in a general sense.*

For the author of 2 Timothy, "scripture" (*graphē*) is a reference to the Old Testament. At the time 2 Timothy was written, there was not yet a New Testament, although some of Paul's early letters were likely circulating, and perhaps also a couple of the canonical gospels. So when the author of 2 Timothy writes that "all scripture is inspired by God," he is referring to what Christians now think of as the Old Testament. To take this as a statement that applies to our modern Bibles is to make it mean something the author could not have meant.

What does it mean to call something "inspired"? Naming something as inspired is a way of saying it is not average but rather rises above the ordinary to move us emotionally or to fundamentally shift the way we see the world and what might be possible.

* See Mark 12:35–37, which cites Psalm 110.

Imagine a churchgoer saying to the preacher after the service, "Thank you, your sermon today was inspired!" Now if you've been a regular preacher you might be rolling your eyes at this point, as these things rarely happen (but we can all dream). But in this imaginative exercise, such a comment would not be a claim that the preacher was verbalizing the direct words of God as they were dictated to him or her, nor would it be a claim that the sermon was perfect or without error. Rather, it's a way of saying the sermon really connected, that it rose above the everyday noise of life and spoke in a way that cut through. It is a way of saying, "I heard a message from God in what you said," or, "I had a sense of the divine speaking to me in the sermon." We can equally experience this kind of inspired connection with the divine through beautiful music and art, in nature, through conversation with a wise friend, or through a whole range of God's other good gifts to us.

We might think of the inspired nature of Scripture in a similar way. It conveys to us the message of the divine through human agents, and in that message are profound truths about the nature of God and the way God has acted and promises to act in the world. Inspiration has multiple dimensions. We might say the authors of the Bible were inspired by their experiences of God, but they were also compelled to write in the hope of inspiring others to faith or moral behavior. Readers are inspired when they connect with these words in a way that is meaningful. Just as in the sermon example above, inspiration occurs in the dynamic interaction between the Bible and the reader, between tradition and a new situation.*

The difference between biblical inspiration and the general inspiration that we might attribute to any other artistic endeavor is that Christians acknowledge the Holy Spirit as an active participant in these various moments of inspiration. When early

---

* David R. Law, *Inspiration of the Scriptures* (London: Continuum, 2001), 132.

Christians wrote about Scripture being inspired, they were conveying a sense that these texts spoke about God in particular ways that made sense of Jesus's death and resurrection. They assumed that the Holy Spirit was involved. And yes, that made it trustworthy and true.

The weight of interpretation of 2 Timothy 3:16 has been on the inspired nature of the Scriptures with far less regard for the other half of the equation. Verses 16–17 continue: "All scripture is inspired by God and is useful for teaching, for reproof, for correction, and for training in righteousness so that everyone who belongs to God may be proficient, equipped for every good work." That is, Scripture might be divinely inspired, but its practical and ethical application is what interests the author here. He is addressing the recipients' conduct in this part of the letter, not writing a doctrine of Scripture. To claim biblical inspiration on the basis of one line in a larger argument that is actually about good conduct is overly simplistic and potentially reads something into the Scriptures that was never intended.

This attempt to put 2 Timothy 3:16 in its context is not a rejection of the idea that Scripture is inspired by God. Indeed, this is the way the majority of Christian apostles, priests, disciples, and scholars have spoken about Scripture, although the language and nuance might differ. I am, however, questioning the idea that inspiration means God dictated the Bible word for word. Nowhere does the Bible claim it was divinely dictated in that way.*

That these various texts written by different people in different contexts testify to a faithful, liberating God who chooses to be in partnership with humanity speaks to the way the authors' own lives have been shaped by the experience of God. That experience of the divine is what inspired them to write the stories, share laws that shape communities in God's ways, devise psalms of praise

* There is one claim in Scripture that God wrote, but only in reference to the Ten Commandments (see Exod. 24:12; Deut. 5:22).

24

and lament, and speak with hope about a better future. As we shall see, their experience of God also inspired them to update and interpret previous Scriptures. As 2 Timothy says, such inspiration ideally prompts us to do "every good work" (2 Tim. 3:17).

Inerrant and Infallible

Being inspired is frequently equated with being infallible or inerrant when people talk about the Bible, but these words do not mean the same thing. *Inerrant* means "without error" and *infallible* means "incapable of error." It is worth noting at the outset that the Bible nowhere uses these terms to refer to itself nor claims to be without error. These terms have, unfortunately in my view, become identity markers in modern Christianity although they mean slightly different things in evangelical Christianity than they do in fundamentalist expressions of Christian faith (noting there can be overlap between these two groups). For that reason, I am going to take a bit of time to address them.

An ancient view of inerrancy claims that the original Greek or Hebrew of the biblical text is inerrant but human interpretation and translation are not.* While we do not have an "original" Bible, this view points to a belief that what God communicates is perfect but acknowledges that human mediation, communication, copying, and translation are not. There is a great deal of variation in how this is expressed, but even ancient Christians like Augustine, who referred to the Bible as being "without error," acknowledged that it contained grammatical and historical mistakes and therefore presumably did not mean without error in every single regard.

By the nineteenth and twentieth centuries, claims of inerrancy were most often used by those appealing to biblical au-

---

* See, for example, Augustine, *Letters of Saint Augustine* 82.1.3, in *The Nicene and Post-Nicene Fathers of the Christian Church*, series 1, vol. 1, ed. Philip Schaff (Grand Rapids: Eerdmans, 1994), 348.

thority to support slavery, creationism, or hierarchical gender roles. In other words, as society was changing, perceived threats to the status quo (be they from scientists like Charles Darwin, abolitionists, or feminists) led some church leaders to become more narrow as they sought to defend biblical authority as well as their own.* The scholar Angela Parker, for example, argues that the doctrines of inerrancy and infallibility of the Bible are deeply tied to white supremacy and the desire of the white church to control interpretation in an authoritarian way.†

Many contemporary Christians, perhaps unaware of this history, have been taught that inerrancy is the correct belief about the Bible and that it applies to everything in the Bible. They therefore consider the Bible to be the supreme authority on everything—science and history as well as theology. Such a stance puts faith at odds with scientific and historical scholarship, pitting belief in a creator God against evolution, and rejecting contemporary medical insights on matters of gender or sexuality. This makes the Bible into something it never claims to be and potentially results in rejecting the gifts of God that come to us through scientific discovery.

This view also sets up unnecessary conflicts. One can affirm God as Creator and believe that God used the process of evolution to create, for example. Even Christians who claim they believe the Bible is inerrant in everything are likely to vaccinate their children against smallpox, drive a car (although the Bible says nothing about vaccines or cars), or go to a doctor rather than a faith healer when their child breaks a leg. This suggests there are limits to biblical inerrancy in the actual practice of those who might profess it.

* Thanks to Kate Hanch for sharing an unpublished paper with me that traces the ways slave owners appealed to inerrancy to defend slavery as biblical. The paper argues such a move was not in keeping with the reformers' views on Scripture.

† Angela Parker, *If God Still Breathes, Why Can't I? Black Lives Matter and Biblical Authority* (Grand Rapids: Eerdmans, 2021), 5–8.

We humans are capable of discerning that there are matters for which we need to turn to the Bible and matters for which we turn to modern medicine and that they do not have to contradict one another. For this reason, some Christian churches have sought to nuance inerrancy's scope by saying the Bible is inerrant for matters of faith and salvation but acknowledging that it is not a science book, was written long before the modern scientific era, and should not therefore be considered without error on those matters.* This clarification rejects the kind of fundamentalism that puts the Bible in conflict with other areas of knowledge, yet still privileges the Bible on matters of faith.

Some Christian traditions do not use language of inerrancy at all, some limit its scope to matters of faith, and some do claim inerrancy in all matters (as described above). Its most dangerous form, however, is found among those who argue for biblical inerrancy but conflate inerrancy of the text with inerrancy of *their* interpretation. This becomes highly problematic. Let us take the example of 1 Timothy 2:12, which can be translated in the following way(s): "I permit no woman (wife) to teach or have authority over (give orders to) a man (husband)" (NRSV with translation options in parentheses).

Christians who hold a complementarian view of gender (that God intended for men and women to have different roles, with men leading and women submitting) argue that this view is inherent to the Bible. So their interpretation of 1 Timothy 2:12, "I permit no woman (wife) to teach or dominate (have total power over) a man (husband)," means no Christian women can teach or hold a

* For example, the Second Vatican Council's *Dei Verbum* clarified that Scripture was inerrant on matters of faith and theology but not history or science. Vatican II Council, "Dogmatic Constitution on Divine Revelation: *Dei verbum*." Solemnly promulgated by His Holiness Pope Paul VI on November 18, 1965. https://www.vatican.va/archive/hist_councils/ii_vatican_council/documents/vat-ii_const_19651118_dei-verbum_en.html. Accessed October 5, 2021.

position of authority, such as being a minister, over Christian men. In this interpretation, women cannot preach or lead Bible study to mixed audiences, but they might be allowed to teach other women (usually under male authority) or Sunday school.

Yet the text invites questions this interpretation does not account for: What did it mean to "teach" in that context? Is the author reflecting cultural norms or challenging them? If it reflects cultural norms about the roles of women two thousand years ago, do we need to accept those cultural norms as God's eternal truth? Did the author have in mind any kind of teaching or just theology? That is, should we interpret this as a ban on women teaching anything in society—literature, math, chemistry—or just Christian faith? And if it is just Christian faith (as most complementarians claim), then is preaching teaching? Is Sunday school teaching? Is leading a Bible study teaching? If teaching is associated with having authority, is there a way to teach without having dominance over someone, and would that be allowed? How one answers each of these questions involves making decisions about interpretation. Yet in some conservative churches there is only one acceptable answer: women cannot preach and teach faith to adult men. If you challenge that, you will be told you are challenging the inerrancy of Scripture when in fact you are challenging one interpretation of Scripture and no human interpretation is without error or infallible.

The irony is that those who hold fast to the idea that the Bible is inerrant and infallible claim to be holding the Scriptures in the highest regard, yet nowhere in the Bible does it refer to itself in this way. These ideas are alien to the Scriptures themselves and are later doctrines with their own long, polemical history. As David Law writes, "The most powerful argument against biblical inerrancy, however, is that it fails to do justice to the phenomena of the Bible."* To claim the Bible is inerrant and infallible is to

---

* Law, *Inspiration of the Scriptures*, 89. Law cites various discrepancies

put a category onto Scripture that is of human making. It is not accepting the Bible for what it is.

I do not believe the Bible is inerrant or infallible. I believe it is inspired by God (in the sense above) and that God worked with and through human beings to communicate God's message. Because God chose to work through humans, the Bible itself is infused with cultural limitations and human bias as well as human imagination and creativity. Humans, no matter how spiritually in tune with God or inspired by the Spirit they are, are always limited by the language and ideas of their culture. I believe that while the core theological truth might be "inerrant" (if using such a word is helpful to describe a theological truthfulness), the Bible is messy, human, and unclear in places, and I think it is all the more interesting for it. Throughout this book I hope to show you why.

God Lets Humans Tell the Story

That God lets humans tell God's story is a paraphrase of something biblical scholar Pete Enns wrote that neatly captures the human dynamic of the Bible.* It is deeply theologically important that God chooses to work in this way. When the Bible speaks of God's interaction with humanity, it speaks of a God who relies on humans to work with God. The ultimate example of this is the incarnation: God entrusted the Son to human parents, a Son who was himself fully human and who in turn

---

in the Bible, such as how Matthew 27:9–10 claims to be quoting Jeremiah when it is quoting Zechariah 11:12–13 or how 2 Samuel 24:1–2 conflicts with 1 Chronicles 21:1–2.

  * Peter Enns, *The Bible Tells Me So: Why Defending Scripture Has Made Us Unable to Read It* (New York: HarperOne, 2015), 231. Enns writes, "The Bible looks the way it does because 'God lets his children tell the story,' so to speak." He refers to the limited perspective children have when it comes to describing what their parents are doing.

called disciples to help him in his mission and to continue it after his death and resurrection. The 1965 Catholic statement on Scripture puts it like this: "For the words of God, expressed in human language, have been made like human discourse, just as the word of the eternal Father, when He took to Himself the flesh of human weakness, was in every way made like men."*

The God revealed in Jesus Christ is incarnational, a God who chose to "become flesh" in Jesus (John 1:14) in order to communicate with us, save us, and be in relationship with us. This is the God that Scripture consistently reveals. From the beginning of the biblical story, God chooses humans as co-workers: women and men are entrusted to care for creation (Gen. 1:28); Adam is asked to name all that God made (Gen. 2:19–20); Noah saves creation from the flood (Gen. 7); Abraham and Sarah carry God's blessing to the world (Gen. 12); Moses is asked to rescue a people and speak for God to them (Exod. 3:7–12; 19:19–25); the prophet Micah reminds the people they are called to be just; Ezekiel reminds them God is with them in a foreign land; Jonah is asked to speak the hope of redemption to his enemies; Mary is entrusted with the wellbeing of Go[...] Luke 1:26–38); Peter is commissioned to care for Jesus's f[...] hn 21:15–17); and the women disciples are entrusted with [...] s of Jesus's resurrection (Mark 16:7; Luke 24:9). There a[...] tless other examples, but the point is God calls human[...] ctive participants in God's mission, even with all our fl[...]

None of the people named abo[...] entirely right. Peter denies Jesus three times when face[...] danger; Jonah tries to run away from his task and has a mas[...] e hissy fit about the fact that God is merciful to his enemies; Abraham and Sarah lie repeatedly (he pretends his wife is his sister); and in Mark's Gospel, the women commissioned to testify about Jesus's empty tomb

* Vatican II Council, "Dogmatic Constitution on Divine Revelation: *Dei verbum*" (November 18, 1965), ch. 3, par. 13.

run away in fear. Yet still God chooses humans. God chooses us to be co-workers in prophecy, in testimony, in justice, in caring for the world, and in giving voice to that partnership as well as telling of the redemption God offers as recorded in the Bible. God lets humans tell God's story.

What about Authority?

Reverence for the Bible can be a lovely thing, but it also leads people to treat the Bible in strange and contradictory ways. When I was a lecturer at a reformed theological seminary in North America, I encountered a number of students from very conservative Christian backgrounds. I would start my introductory class by asking them how the Bible was treated in their homes, as this helped me understand where they were coming from. Some students did not grow up with a Bible, but for many the family Bible was something that sat on a shelf or in a locked cabinet; it was treated with reverence and respect as a kind of holy object and only brought out on special occasions. The family Bible was something one did not play with as a child and children were not allowed to touch it without permission. I would then show them my English-language Bible—a beaten-up NRSV held together with packing tape. I have had it since I started seminary at age twenty and it has moved houses and continents with me about eleven times since then. So, for sentimental reasons, I just keep taping it up to hold it together rather than buying a new one. Inside this beaten up Bible, writing is cramped in the margins, words are underlined or crossed out (mostly where I think the translation is poor), and various pages have coffee or tea stains. When I show students my Bible, someone is always shocked. The coffee and tea stains particularly grate on those who have been taught to treat the Bible with reverence because it is a holy book. How could you rest your coffee cup on the Holy Bible? But is reverence for the authority of the Bible best enacted by leaving a Bible closed on a shelf, albeit pristine, or is reverence for this book best shown in stained and worn pages? If the Bible is authoritative, why and what does that mean for how we treat it?

The idea that the Bible is inspired by God through the Holy Spirit is often the key claim to its authority for people of faith. Yet this conflates inspiration and authority. What imbues the Christian Bible with authority is that the church community decided these particular books have special status,* that they are unique, trustworthy, and testify to the Word of God (that is, Jesus). It is not that the Bible contains the only ancient texts that speak about God or Jesus—there are tons of others.

The process that led to the formation of a "canon," an agreed-upon list of sacred texts, was long and complex. In the first few centuries after Jesus, early Christian texts started to circulate in collections. The earliest such collection was probably the letters of Paul, then the gospels, and so on. By the second century CE we find Christians referencing particular texts that were read aloud in worship—texts included in what we now know to be in the Bible. In large part, the Bible was born out of what communities of faith found useful, inspiring, or important to read. The canon was formed by the practices of early Christian communities as much as it was by church councils.

The other part of the story involved power and politics. As churches became more institutional and leaders emerged in the form of bishops, councils of the church met to determine doctrine and theological matters. By the late fourth century CE, the Christian biblical canon was all but determined. Because of the way they speak about God and the apostolic authority of

---

* John Webster, *Word and Church: Essays in Christian Dogmatics* (Edinburgh: T&T Clark, 2001), 112.

those who wrote them, these texts were set apart as the sacred or holy texts of Christianity and of divine self-manifestation. One can, of course, see the Holy Spirit at work in the discernment of these communities as we hope the Holy Spirit is at work in all church decision-making, but that is a belief, not a historical or provable fact.

CONCLUSION

In this chapter, we have seen that the modern Bible we have in our homes and churches is in fact a collection of writings produced by different humans over thousands of years. These writings have survived in many ancient manuscripts and have been translated by teams of editors and translators. "The Bible" therefore is not a singular entity. This awareness can be discomforting. Can we trust that what we have in our hands is true?

For me, believing the Bible and living under its authority is a choice I make as a follower of Jesus. It is a choice to sit under the discipline of the Christian tradition, which has determined that the Bible, in all its different forms, witnesses to God's grace in a unique way. As theologian Philip Ziegler writes, the Bible is "diverse human witness to the incomparable uniqueness and salutary concreteness of the living God."* It is by faith, then, that I accept that these texts testify to the Word of God (Jesus), are true, and are therefore useful for learning how to be the person God created me to be as well as how to serve God. I do not believe *in* the Bible (as an object). I *believe* the Bible (as a testimony). I believe the Bible is true and it is authoritative for those who call themselves Christians.

* Philip G. Ziegler, "On the Present Possibility of *Sola Scriptura*," *International Journal of Systematic Theology* (2022): 19.

In the next chapter we will address the question of why we need to interpret at all. Why can't we just read the words on the page? We will examine the various references to interpretation within the Bible itself and, in the chapters that follow, discover the ways that biblical writers interpret their own scriptures. As we do so, the goal is to let the Bible speak on its own terms.

CHAPTER TWO

Bible Interpreting Bible

So they read from the book, from the law of God,
with interpretation. They gave the sense so that
the people understood the reading.

— NEHEMIAH 8:8

I hated English class in high school, particularly when we got to Shakespeare in the curriculum. Every year there was at least one Shakespeare play to read in English and every year I found it tedious. Don't get me wrong, I loved to read, often devouring novels by flashlight under the duvet after my mother had told me for the umpteenth time to turn off my light and go to sleep (Kindles and tablets did not yet exist). But being forced to analyze and dissect texts took the joy out of it for me. My particular resistance to Shakespeare, however, was because it was hard work and, although it was supposedly written in English, I couldn't understand the words or the jokes. The different and strange language of Shakespearean plays made me want to reject them and also made them seem irrelevant to my life.

The reality is most of us need help to understand the puns and strange words in a Shakespeare play or sonnet. Without training we cannot just pick it up and read it in the way we can read Harry Potter or a John Grisham novel. The English language has changed rather dramatically in the almost five hundred years since Shakespeare wrote, and so we need context to understand the politics, gender norms, puns, and culture of his time. If this is true for Shakespeare, how much more so for a text that is two thousand years old and was written in a completely different language?

In the New Testament letter known as 2 Peter, the author refers to Paul's letters by rather amusingly writing "there are

some things in them that are hard to understand" (2 Peter 3:16).*
As someone who also finds some of Paul's letters difficult, I sym-
pathize! Paul's letters can be very hard to understand. Peter's
main concern in this passage is that when Scriptures are hard
to understand, they can be twisted to mean things they do not,
and he rails against "ignorant and unstable" people who do such
things. Paul's letters are, rather astonishingly, grouped with "the
rest of the Scriptures." While it is interesting that Paul's writings were considered to have such high status so early on, that
is not the main point here. In acknowledging that different interpretations of difficult Bible passages are possible, this early
Christian writer is acknowledging that the Scriptures require
interpretation because their meaning is not always obvious *and*
that the Scriptures can be made to mean things they do not. It
is perhaps not surprising then that Christians have been arguing
over interpretation ever since.

In this chapter we will look at why we need to interpret and
the things that make biblical interpretation complex. Along the
way we will begin to unpack some of the ways the Bible itself
talks about interpretation.

Why Interpret?

"The Bible says . . ." is a frequently used phrase and yet one that
is clearly problematic when we consider the traditions that lie
behind the modern translation of the book in our hands. It is

---

* Many scholars think that 2 Peter is written by a later Christian
using the name Peter as a pseudonym. That he refers to Paul's letters in
hindsight is one reason for dating this as a late first-century letter. For
convenience I will be referring to the author as Peter, but I do not think
it likely that this was written by the apostle Peter.

not that the Bible does not and cannot speak with a clear voice, but rather that we need to do a bit of work to discern that voice in the same way that we constantly interpret spoken and written words in everyday life (mostly unconsciously).

In the previous chapter, I wrote about letting the Bible speak on its own terms. That is, to let the Bible be itself and not something we might want it to be, whether that's a moral code, a rule book, a sourcebook for all knowledge, a scientific textbook, something entirely human, or something free of human agency and error. In advocating that we let the Bible speak on its own terms, I was addressing the nature and function of the Bible— what it is and what it is not. I wrote about the ways the Bible as a historical text is messy and complex; it is a compilation of numerous texts by different authors addressing a range of contexts and written over a long period of time in at least two languages. I also acknowledged that the Bible as Scripture is the sacred text of the Christian church, a text that Christians believe speaks about God in a unique way and that therefore has a particular authority. Its function is to point us to God.

When I was a newly ordained twenty-four-year-old, my first congregational placement was a cluster of churches in rural Victoria, Australia. As the "young" minister, I was tasked with preparing teenagers for confirmation. The first time I did this we had a group of about six teenagers aged between fourteen and sixteen years old. Most of them had grown up in the church, but there wasn't a strong culture of Bible study or cell groups, so I decided to use Luke's Gospel as the heart of their confirmation preparation. Each week they had to read two to three chapters of Luke and we'd discuss what they noticed and learned about Jesus and being a disciple. The idea was they would read an entire gospel in preparation for confirmation. For some of them, it was the first time they had done so. A few weeks in, I asked as usual, "What did you notice when you read Luke this week?" You could have heard a pin drop when one young woman said in a sheepish tone: "Jesus wasn't very nice."

The observation that Jesus wasn't always nice, from a young woman whose family and church had taught her that the best expression of Christian faith was niceness, was brave and life changing. It is also the kind of observation that will come only when you let the biblical text speak for itself in an environment that is safe, open, and encouraging of genuine questions. Such an observation, though, is not the end but rather the beginning of a conversation. Once one has observed that by white, middle-class, Protestant standards, Jesus was not always "nice," one has to grapple with what to do with that. This is where interpretation comes in. In that class we explored Luke's cultural norms versus our own. We examined what is going on in the passage and its literary context to see the larger point. We were prepared to have our theology challenged by the Bible and let go of preconceived notions of the divine that no longer fit, or at least question where they came from. We needed to accept that the gospel writers present a Jesus who is complex and behaves differently at different times and that perhaps the Jesus they presented did not behave much like the ideal young male (white) pastor in the contemporary church. We even examined whether "niceness" is a Christian virtue at all. When we did all those things, a deeper, more nuanced, more adult faith emerged as we began to see Jesus removed from the whitewashing and domestication of so much of the institutional church. But all of this starts from an honest observation about the text that lets it speak on its own terms.

Letting the Bible be what it is does not remove the need for interpretation. Interpretation is inevitable and unavoidable. Some of you might be wondering why we can't just read the words on the page of the Bible. Some will appeal to the "plain sense" of Scripture, the idea that we can just take the words on the pages of the Bible at face value. But even when we do this, we are interpreting. Every act of reading is an act of interpretation. To then read for the "plain sense" is choosing to interpret in a "plain sense" kind of way. Equally, to read it literally is to choose to interpret the Bible with a specific lens, one I would argue is not inherent to the Bible. Intuitively most of us know that the diversity of the Bible's genres means that we read certain parts differently: the rhetoric of a letter exhorting ethical behavior functions differently from the poetry of the Psalms. To read the Bible on its own terms is to recognize what it is and how it functions at each of these moments. The simple fact is that as soon as we read anything, we are already interpreting, that is, trying to make sense of it. And if we are reading the Bible in English, we are already reading someone else's interpretation because we are reading a translation, which is shaped by the translator's theological preferences and cultural biases. Interpretation is unavoidable.

As the Bible is central to Christian faith, much is at stake in interpreting it well.* So while it might seem contradictory to be advocating for both letting the Bible speak on its own terms and the need to interpret it, these two things are not mutually exclusive. Indeed, the one informs the other because as long as we try to make the Bible something it is not, we will try to interpret it in ways that are foreign to it. Or to put it more positively, the nature of the Bible as a witness to God told by God's children over hundreds of years has implications for interpretation. But first let us look at some of the things that make biblical interpretation complex.

Words Vary in Meaning

Thirty years ago, if someone said "it's in the cloud," you might have looked up to the sky, perhaps expecting to see a bird or airplane. Now our thoughts go to that mysterious place where all our electronic data is backed up and stored. The word *cloud* has multiplied in meaning, and future interpreters will need to use context to determine which of these senses is being evoked.

---

* Despite the range of theological views within worldwide Christianity, the Bible holds a central place in all traditions. However, different denominations also appeal to different sources of authority, such as tradition, reason, experience, spiritual revelation, ecclesial authority, and so on.

As well as adapting words, cultures also invent words. A modern example is the verb *to google*, which is now officially listed in the Oxford Dictionary. Even twenty years ago, we could not have imagined saying "I googled it." Can we assume then that in 500 or 1,500 years' time, someone will understand that it refers to a specific company's search engine but became generic for looking up something on the internet? Maybe.

Such shifts in language apply not only to technological terms like *google, tweet, zoom, tablet,* and *cloud,* but also to other words, like *gay, ghost, wicked, sick, fulsome, nonplussed,* and *hot.* Language is constantly changing, which makes reading anything old a more complex task.

Take a simple word like *fear,* which appears in the Bible over four hundred times. In many of these cases, *fear* indicates what it does in common English—terror, alarm, or anxiety over something negative or life threatening. But there are also numerous times that fear in the Bible actually means something more like awe or reverence for God leading to worship (e.g., Prov. 9:10; Ps. 33:8–9). When we see this word in context, we can usually work out which sense is meant, but that itself is an act of interpretation.

Sodomite is another example of the way language changes. A historically accurate sense of the word would be a rapist or wicked person, but that is probably not what comes to mind for most readers. In Genesis 19, Sodom is the town where Lot lives, a town that already has a reputation for being wicked. When Lot receives two (angelic) visitors, the menfolk surround his house and demand that Lot send them out to be gang raped. It is a horrific story. In the ancient world, offering hospitality was offering protection. What the townsfolk demand contravenes so many moral standards but especially the standard of hospitality. That Lot offers his daughters to the rapists in an effort to protect the visitors indicates something of the nature of hospitality and the valuing of male life over female life at the time. The story ends with God rescuing Lot's family and destroying Sodom for its horrific violence.

In the original story, the term *sodomite* refers to a man of Sodom and nothing else. Sodom (along with Gomorrah) is repeatedly mentioned in the Bible as an example of God's judgment on wickedness.* In Ezekiel, for example, the "sin of Sodom" is that it did not aid those in need when it had an excess of food. Nowhere in the Old Testament is Sodom associated specifically with homosexual behavior.† Despite this, sodomy became synonymous with homosexuality in later Christian tradition and continues to be used in this sense well into the twenty-first century in both common speech and laws relating to LGBTIQ+ folk.‡ The sin of the Sodomites had nothing to do with their sexual orientation (which we do not know) and everything to do with their desire to gang rape visitors to their town—a sign of their extreme wickedness. Yet because the intended victims were male in the original story, *sodomite* became a derogatory term for anyone who engaged in anal sex, and it is now almost impossible for us to hear the term without this resonance.

In the first example, we saw how the same word (*fear*) can have a different sense within the Bible itself. In the second example, we have seen how language can change and take on a resonance of its own that has little to do with the original biblical meaning. Words vary in meaning depending on context and can morph into something quite different over time. Both of these

* For example, see Isaiah 1:9–10; Jeremiah 23:14; Ezekiel 16:46–48; Matthew 10:15; Romans 9:29.

† There is one possible exception in Jude 7, although it is ambiguous and it is hard to know what kind of sexual immorality is meant there. The earliest reference to Sodom being used specifically to indicate anal rape occurs in 2 Enoch, a text that dates to about the first century CE, like the New Testament. Second Enoch 10 speaks of the punishments that await "child corruption in the anus in the manner of Sodom." It is noteworthy that the reference to children indicates an act of rape, not consensual adult sex.

‡ Queensland, one of Australia's states, removed the word *sodomy* from their laws only in 2016. https://www.abc.net.au/news/2016-09-16 /why-is-the-word-sodomy-offensive/7852736.

affect how we read the simple words on the pages of our Bibles, and we need to be careful we are not reading back into the text something that was never there.

Cultural Context Matters

Words and phrases can also have different meanings depending on the context. The dramatic "I want to die" from a teenager to her friend on discovering her mother has picked her up from school in an embarrassing outfit is quite different from the "I want to die" whispered to a nurse in the palliative care ward as a patient rejects further medical intervention. Context means we might treat one of these utterances with an eye-roll and the other with the greatest empathy.

Many people can and do open the Bible, read what is on the page, and feel that the Bible speaks to them. Such readers find meaning in the simple act of reading. I am not critiquing this nor questioning the profound experiences people have with God when reading the Bible in this devotional way. I do, however, believe that the Bible can have *more* meaning when readers are able to pick up cultural references or understand the symbolic language. There is a lot we miss, or worse, get wrong about God and God's people when we read without attention to language, context, and culture.

A classic biblical example is "an eye for an eye." The full verse reads:

> Anyone who maims another shall suffer the same injury in return: fracture for fracture, eye for eye, tooth for tooth; the injury inflicted is the injury to be suffered. (Lev. 24:19–20)

This law from Leviticus 24 seems terribly harsh to modern ears. It conjures images of a God who is vengeful and a society more brutal and retributive than our own. Yet if we look at this teaching in its context, we discover a profound element of justice in this passage.

In 1901, archaeologists discovered a stone stele with laws carved into it. Known as the Code of Hammurabi, it contains a set of laws very similar to biblical laws, but they are the laws of ancient Babylon. The stele is on display at the Louvre in Paris. The Code of Hammurabi is older than Leviticus, giving us insight into what the surrounding cultures' laws were and a point of comparison for the laws we find in the Pentateuch. It also gives us a sense of the kinds of values that Israelites embodied that set them apart from other cultures and other religions. What we discover in the Code of Hammurabi are some similarities to Leviticus as well as clear differences. A parallel law to Leviticus 24 in the Code of Hammurabi states,

> If a man destroy the eye of another man, they shall destroy his eye. [An eye for an eye.]
> If one break a man's bone, they shall break his bone.
> If one destroy the eye of a freeman, or break the bone of a freeman, he shall pay one mana of silver.
> If one destroy the eye of a man's slave, or break the bone of a man's slave, he shall pay one-half of his price. (Code of Hammurabi 196–200)*

In the Babylonian equivalent of an "eye for an eye," retributive justice is only for men of equal elite status under the law. If an elite male injures another elite male, he suffers the same fate. But if an elite male injures a freedman (a former slave), he simply pays a fine. In the third part of the law, if an elite male injures a slave, the fine is only half the amount, and it is paid to the slave's owner as damages for breaking his "property." Babylonian law had a tiered system of retributive justice depending on the perceived value of the victim.

---

* Robert Harper, *The Code of Hammurabi, King of Babylon, about 2250 B.C.* (Chicago: University of Chicago Press, 1904), 73–75.

When we reread Leviticus 24 in light of the Code of Hammurabi, its equity is striking. In the theology of Leviticus, all human life, be it male, female, slave, free, citizen, or foreigner, is treated the same because it has the same value to God. What at first appears barbaric and harsh—an eye for an eye—is actually a profound and radical statement of human equality in its ancient context. Without knowledge of the Ancient Near Eastern cultures that surrounded the Hebrew people or of comparative law codes, we can easily miss the distinctive theological affirmation of all humanity in this passage. While I don't think we should base contemporary laws on a literal application of Leviticus 24:19–20, the deeper theological affirmation that all life is of equal value to God is something we hopefully still want to uphold when it comes to justice and restitution.

We Can't Always Recover Authorial Intent

Another factor that makes biblical interpretation complex is that we don't have access to the authors or to the responses of their first readers. We can't check our interpretation with them. In the modern age, most of us are all too familiar with the way communication can be misunderstood. This is particularly true for the written word in the form of text messages or emails. I remember having to explain to a much older colleague that writing in ALL CAPS is considered shouting in an email. He thought he was being helpful as he found capital letters easier to see! Obvious misunderstandings aside, when we write to others our tone can get lost, assumptions are made, and before too long a clumsily worded sentence causes offense. Once the words leave our phone (or tablet or computer), we hand them over to someone else to interpret. Control is likewise handed over, as meaning is made in readers' minds as they interact with our words.

The challenge of having one's words interpreted and misinterpreted was all too familiar to the apostle Paul. Paul wrote many of the letters in the New Testament, but it is his correspondence with the Corinthian community that reveals his own struggles with the way others interpreted his words. The letter we know as 1 Corinthians in the New Testament was not the first letter Paul wrote to the Corinthian church. Sadly, his earlier correspondence is lost. Paul, however, refers to this earlier letter explicitly in 1 Corinthians 5:9, writing, "I wrote to you in my letter not to associate with sexually immoral persons."* He does so to clarify what he meant in his earlier letter: that this instruction was not about avoiding everyone in society (because this is impossible) but rather to avoid other Christ followers who are sexually immoral, drunkards, or robbers. In other words, Paul makes clear that his concern is for the behavior of other Christians and holding them accountable for their actions rather than judging those outside the community (1 Cor. 5:12). That judgment is left to God.

That Paul needs to clarify his earlier letter indicates that it has been misinterpreted and the recipients have come to a conclusion he did not intend when writing it. He does something similar in 1 Corinthians 6:12, building on a previous statement, "all things are lawful," with the new insight that just because things are lawful does not mean they are beneficial. He seeks to limit and clarify a statement that might have led some to revel in their freedoms just a bit too much. Immoral behavior still has consequences in Paul's view, so he qualifies what he had previously written.

While it can be fun to try and guess what any particular biblical author meant when writing, we cannot always recover authorial intent. What we do have are the words on the page, the compiled written record shaped by the communities who kept and copied it. These words demand that we wrestle with

* Margaret M. Mitchell, *Paul and the Emergence of Christian Textuality: Early Christian Literary Culture in Context* (Tübingen: Mohr Siebeck, 2017), 162. Mitchell calls this "the inauguration of Pauline interpretation itself."

them and try to make sense of them. This includes trying to understand what the original author might have meant but also acknowledging we can never perfectly know that. If Paul's first readers, who shared his culture and worldview, could misunderstand him, how much greater is the chance that we might?

Navigating the Gap

A further issue that makes interpretation difficult at times is that twenty-first-century Christians have two thousand years of tradition and interpretation lying between us and the Bible. While some of these traditions are wonderful, some are unhelpful as they reflect the bias of earlier eras, and others are just wrong.

Not long ago I asked my New Testament class what they knew about Pharisees. I wanted to see if I needed to provide some historical context for the passage we were examining. "They were hypocrites," came the first reply from a student. Wrong, but not his fault. If you look up the word *Pharisee* in a major dictionary, like the *Oxford English Dictionary*, one of the definitions offered is "hypocrite."

Historically, Pharisees were one branch of ancient Judaism known for their strict adherence to the Law (Torah).* The apostle Paul was a Pharisee before becoming a Jesus follower.† Many scholars think Pharisees preceded the rabbinic tradition since they were known for their teaching. In the gospels, however, Pharisees are often portrayed in opposition to Jesus, leading him to call them "hypocrites" at times for not meeting their own demanding standards (e.g., Matt. 23:13–29). In sermons and

---

* See the recent book by Joseph Sievers and Amy-Jill Levine, eds., *The Pharisees* (Grand Rapids: Eerdmans, 2021), which offers a comprehensive historical study of the Pharisees as well as of the references to them in the New Testament and in later Christian tradition.

† Philippians 3:5 (Acts 23:6).

commentaries, this characterization of Pharisees as hypocrites became widespread. In normalizing what is actually a highly contextual criticism of some Pharisees, Christian tradition has directly influenced the dictionary definition, leading to a common misconception that still prevails today about a group in ancient Judaism. We have to unlearn this bias when reading to recognize that while Jesus judged some Pharisees (and scribes and others) to be hypocritical at times, *Pharisee* and *hypocrite* are not synonymous terms.

Another classic example of an interpretive tradition that needs to be unlearned is that of the word *helper* in Genesis 2:18. In this creation story, God has made the first human (the *adam*, literally meaning "the earthling") and now proclaims that it needs "a helper."* In the old King James Version, the translation was "help-meet." Now, *helper* can mean a range of things and does not necessarily imply subordination, although it could. For example, friends help friends as equals; parents can help their children, and a child can help an ageing or sick parent; bosses help employees, and employees help bosses. Helping by itself does not mean the person helping is lesser; indeed, in some instance the helper might be the more powerful or senior person. Yet in the history of interpretation, a dominant view has been that because Eve is the "helper," she is inferior in some way to Adam, designed to assist Adam as a subordinate rather than to be his equal. Men have preached this interpretation to (at) me to explain why I should not, as a female, be ordained or a biblical scholar who teaches men. Once upon a time I would have agreed with them.

Now comes the twist. The Hebrew word for helper is *ezer*, and it is used about eighty times in the Old Testament. The vast majority of these times it is used for God, particularly in the

---

* *Adam* is a play on *adamah*, the Hebrew word for earth or dirt. So *adam* is not a proper noun but a way of referring to the first human as an earthling, literally a creature made out of earth.

Psalms, where God is frequently invoked as a helper to the people in their distress (e.g., Gen. 49:25; Isa. 41:13; 50:7; Ps. 30:10).* One of God's characteristics is being a God who helps the people (Ezek. 30:8). When preachers or biblical scholars talk about God as helper, they never imply that this makes God subordinate or lesser in status in some way. Existing theological beliefs about God's power and nature mean that interpreters are extremely unlikely to make that association for the divine. And yet this is what interpreters have done for centuries when it comes to Eve. Preexisting notions about the inferiority of women mean that Eve's being an *ezer* implies subordination. What if, instead, it implied she was like God?

We Bring Ourselves to the Text

Lastly, when we read and interpret the Bible, we do not read in a vacuum, nor do we read as disinterested or objective parties. We bring our own experiences, culture, beliefs, and biases to our reading, and this shapes our interpretation whether we are aware of it or not. We have already seen this in the examples above in terms of the gap between us and the original text. Another classic example of this in the history of biblical interpretation is the case of Junia.

At the end of Paul's letter to the Romans, he sends greetings to a number of people whose names we assume meant something to that community even if we don't know precisely who they are (Rom. 16:3–16). In the middle of the list Paul writes: "Greet Andronicus and Junia, my kin, who were in prison with me; they are outstanding among the apostles." Andronicus and Junia were probably a married couple who worked as a pair in ministry with Paul. Junia is a female name in Greek, and

---

* Sometimes *ezer* is used for warriors or armies who come to people's aid (Josh. 1:14) or to denote one human helping another.

appears as such in hundreds of non-biblical Greek and Latin manuscripts and inscriptions from the ancient world. That Junia was female was taken for granted by Christian commentators through to the medieval period.* But in the thirteenth century, Junia started being referred to as Junias, the male version of the name, despite this name not existing in Paul's time. By the sixteenth century, Junias, a male apostle, was in various translations of the Bible. This trend of making Junia male continued well into the twentieth century, and it has only been in the last few decades that a number of Bibles have changed back to *Junia* (female) on the basis of incontrovertible evidence.†

While we can only guess at the mindset that led men to change *Junia* to *Junias*, assumptions about the gender of apostles and gender roles play a dominant role. It is notable that during the thirteenth century, the scholar who changed *Junia* to *Junias* was part of a Catholic Church that was moving to limit the freedom of nuns by making them permanently cloistered.‡ Similar assumptions that Paul could not possibly be calling a female apostle one of the most "prominent or outstanding of the apostles" underlay later reformation translations that rendered her male. James Dunn points out how our cultural biases influence interpretation in his commentary on Romans, writing that the "assumption that it [the name *Junia*] must be a male is a striking indictment of male presumption regarding the character and structure of ear-

---

* Eldon Jay Epp, *Junia: The First Woman Apostle* (Minneapolis: Fortress, 2005). You can find a summary list of these references here: https://margmowczko.com/junias-junia-julia-romans-167/.

† This includes the NIV, which changed *Junias* back to *Junia* in its 2011 version. The NEB and NRSV both changed back to *Junia* in 1989. For a full list, see Dennis Preato, "Junia, a Female Apostle: An Examination of the Historical Record," *Priscilla Papers* (2019), https://www.cbeinternational.org/resource/article/priscilla-papers-academic-journal/junia-female-apostle-examination-historical.

‡ https://godswordtowomen.org/juniamcdonnell.htm.

liest Christianity."* Even evangelical scholars now acknowledge that Junia is evidence that "women had a key part to play in the ministries of the earliest churches."† Regardless of one's theological views on the leadership of women in the contemporary church, it is incontrovertible that Paul has no qualms calling a woman an apostle and an outstanding one at that.

While our experiences and worldview can shape our reading in ways that prevent us from seeing what is actually in the text, they can also give us profound insights that transform lives and communities. Gerald West is a biblical scholar working in South Africa, where he helped found the Ujamaa Centre dedicated to contextual Bible study that brings about social transformation.‡ It is an approach to biblical interpretation that emerged out of the conflict and trauma of apartheid. One of the core commitments at the Ujamaa Centre is to privilege the lived experience of the poor, working class, and marginalized in reading the Bible. In various papers and talks, West has described how reading the biblical story of the rape of Tamar (2 Sam. 13:1–22) with women who have also experienced sexual violence can be life-giving and transformative for them when done sensitively and with the contextual method Ujamaa has developed. Women who find their story reflected in the biblical story find themselves empowered to speak of their own story—"if this story is in the Bible we will not be silent."§ When readers see their story in the text, they are validated and empowered. Likewise, when read by women who know too well the terror of rape, Tamar's dignity and agency in the story is highlighted, something that happens precisely be-

---

* James D. G. Dunn, *Romans*, vol. 2 (Dallas: Word, 1988), 894.

† Michael F. Bird, *Romans* (Grand Rapids: Zondervan, 2016), 526.

‡ http://ujamaa.ukzn.ac.za/Homepage.aspx.

§ Gerald O. West, "Recovering the Biblical Story of Tamar: Training for Transformation, Doing Development," in *For Better for Worse: The Role of Religion in Development Cooperation* (Halmstad: Swedish Mission Council, 2016), 138.

cause of who the reader is and her experience of the world. Such readings can also help uncover the way the men in the biblical story and the men in one's current story can be allies, bystanders, or abusers in ways that unravel the patriarchal structures at work in gender-based violence and concepts of masculinity. Certain life experiences enable readers to see things in the text others will miss.

I begin my New Testament introductory class each year by asking students to name who they are and what worldviews and assumptions they bring to the text. These include culture, ethnicity, life experience, gender, theological influences, language, and assumptions about what the Bible is. We do this exercise because all of these things will influence what they notice, the kinds of questions they ask, and how they interpret the Bible, so it helps if we start to become aware of them. This is not a bad thing. I believe God wants us to bring our full and true selves to the Scriptures. We just need to be aware that who we are will shape our interpretation. No interpretation is neutral.

Summary

Sometimes in class a student will ask, "What was Jesus thinking when he said . . . ?" If I knew that I could quit my day job! We genuinely want to get to the root of what Jesus or Paul might have been thinking when they did or said something, but there are things we cannot know. For me this means that there should always be a sense of humility to our interpretation of the Bible because, to paraphrase Paul, now we see only dimly (1 Cor. 13:12). This is why most Christian traditions emphasize that in addition to the Bible, we rely on the revelation of the Holy Spirit, the guidance of scholars and priests, and the community around us to aid in understanding what God is communicating to us. In what follows we will see all these aspects at play in the way biblical authors interpret the Bible.

BIBLICAL INTERPRETATION BEGINS IN THE BIBLE

Scholars of the Hebrew Bible or Old Testament have long noted that biblical interpretation begins in the Bible itself. Because the Old Testament was written over hundreds of years, we have later texts that interpret earlier texts in a variety of ways. Michael Fishbane calls this "inner-biblical exegesis."* For us later readers and receivers of the canon, we have inherited the interpretation of the Bible as part of the Bible.

In the next chapter we'll look at the tradition of the Bible rewriting biblical stories, but first we will look at how the Bible itself refers to interpretation, beginning with the prophet Nehemiah.

Nehemiah: Continuity and Discontinuity

One of the earliest explicit references about the need to interpret the Bible comes in Nehemiah. The biblical books of Ezra-Nehemiah tell the story of the Jews returning from exile in Babylon under Persian rule in the late sixth century BCE. Where the Babylonian rulers, having destroyed the Jerusalem temple, had forced many Jews to leave their land and live in Babylon, the Persian rulers permitted Jews to return and even rebuild the temple in Jerusalem. But at least two generations had passed and so the Jews returning to Jerusalem were not the same generation as those who left. Migrants and children of immigrant parents know how quickly generational change can happen as the new generation adapts to their new culture, often clashing with the older generation, who want to keep their traditions. Similar dynamics are at play in the Ezra-Nehemiah story of return.

In one scene, all the returnees gather in the town square in Jerusalem to hear the "book of the law [Torah] of God" read

* Michael Fishbane, *Biblical Interpretation in Ancient Israel* (Oxford: Oxford University Press, 1985), 10.

aloud. This act places the returnees in a long tradition of the public reading of the Torah (see Deut. 31:9–13; 2 Kings 22:8–13; Josh 8:30–35), emphasizing continuity with the tradition. But the author adds a note we do not see in earlier texts—that it was read "with interpretation" and that "they gave the sense so that the people understood the reading" (Neh. 8:8). The implication is that the people could not have understood what was being read aloud without some help.

There has been much debate about the precise meaning of the word *mĕpōrāsh* in 8:8, which can indicate something like interpretation, elucidation, explanation, or translation.* All meanings are possible here. First, the text that was read aloud would have been written in literary Hebrew, and most Jews who had been in exile for a couple of generations would have spoken Aramaic, not formal Hebrew, so it is likely that some actual translation was needed. Second, we see in the Nehemiah text a larger tradition of taking the old law and making it applicable for the new context, that is, interpreting it to show its ongoing relevance and application to their changed historical circumstances. So it is also possible that *mĕpōrāsh* here means "interpretation" or "explanation" in the sense of how it relates to their new circumstances. Whether the exact text Nehemiah refers to as the book of the law of God is the same as our contemporary Torah or Pentateuch is also unclear.† What is clear is that a law book associated with both Moses and God existed at this time and was considered authoritative, but it needed translation and interpretation. As Karen Armstrong writes: "When he [Ezra] expounded the text,

---

* Philip Yoo, "On Nehemiah 8,8a," *Zeitschrift für die Alttestamentliche Wissenschaft* 127, no. 3 (2015): 503–5.

† See Titus Reinmuth, "Nehemiah 8 and the Authority of Torah in Ezra-Nehemiah," in *Unity and Disunity in Ezra-Nehemiah* (Sheffield: Sheffield Phoenix, 2008), 241–62.

the exegete did not reproduce the original Torah imparted in the distant past to Moses but created something new and unexpected. The biblical writers had worked in the same way, radically revising the texts they had inherited. Revelation had not happened once and for all time; it was an ongoing process that could never end, because there was always fresh teaching to be discovered."*

There is another significant aspect to this public reading and interpretation of Scripture. The author of Nehemiah depicts the return of exiles to Jerusalem using metaphors from, and allusions to, the first entry into the land as told in Joshua.† So when the Torah is read to the people, it evokes the time Joshua did the same and renewed the covenant made first with Moses (Josh. 8:30–35). In both settings men, women, and children are present, affirming that God's instruction and covenant is for everyone. The people as a group are mentioned several times throughout this scene, and the author is clear that there is more than one gender in the crowd (8:2–3). Interpreting God's book of the law and seeking to understand it is something done in community, a community inclusive of women and children.

Similarly, there is not just one interpreter in this scene. Rather, the scribe-priest Ezra, the Levites, and another group of named laypeople have a role "helping the people to understand the law" (8:9).‡ Nehemiah 8 affirms that interpretation of God's word is necessary for new contexts, inclusive of the whole

---

* Karen Armstrong, *On the Bible* (Crows Nest, NSW: Allen & Unwin, 2007), 35.

† There are also numerous echoes of Exodus 24 in Nehemiah's account that evoke the first giving of the law.

‡ Twice in this narrative, a named group of different men contribute to either reading the Torah or interpreting it (Neh. 8:4, 7). In both cases there is no mention of their priestly families or scribal training, suggesting they may be laypeople. See G. J. Venema, *Reading Scripture in the Old Testament* (Leiden: Brill, 2004), 168–69.

community, and that interpretation is entrusted to a group, not an individual. In joyful response, the people commit to studying God's word and living it out (8:13).

While Nehemiah's context is very different from that of the contemporary, western Christian church, there are some similarities. We too do not understand the original language and need translation. We too require interpretation to bridge the changed context between our world and our questions and those of the first recipients and producers of the Bible. We can also learn from Nehemiah that study of the Bible takes time and diligence if we really want to understand its message for us and that biblical study is best done in communities that include all and where correct interpretation is not located in just one individual but in a team of qualified leaders. This is not to say one should not read the Bible alone or that doing so cannot be helpful, but when it comes to making sense of the Bible for the community, we need the wisdom of one another to interpret best. Without community and shared wisdom we can end up with cult-like allegiance to one interpretation or one authoritative voice and end up ignoring the voices and perspectives of those who are not in the room.

Nehemiah and New Contexts

Nehemiah also teaches us that new contexts require a new reading of Scripture. The people in Nehemiah were rebuilding their society after terrible war, destruction, and at least two generations in exile. The gulf between those who left and those who stayed would have been huge, requiring translation and new application of biblical teachings.

In the twenty-first century, our goal is not to try to interpret the Bible in the exact same way it was interpreted in 1000 BCE, 200 BCE, or 100 CE, but to recognize that we always need to do the work of applying it to new situations. This is the distinction between exegesis and hermeneutics: to put it simply, exegesis tries to work out the original meaning of a passage, whereas hermeneutics (or interpretation) is more interested in how it applies now. For people of faith, hermeneutics is where the rubber hits the road— what is the Bible saying to me and my community today?

One way to think about this is to think of the Bible, metaphorically, as kernel and chaff. When wheat grows, the kernel is inseparable from the chaff, which protects the seed inside. But only the kernel is edible, so to turn wheat into something nutritious and edible, the chaff has to be removed through a process of threshing and winnowing. Similarly, there are core theological truths in Scripture that are timeless, but the cultural and contextual wrapping (the chaff) needs to be winnowed away to discover the kernel. For example, let's look at Paul's teaching on circumcision.

Whether or not non-Jewish male converts to Christianity had to be circumcised was one of the most controversial issues in earliest Christianity. I suspect it was the ancient church's version of contemporary debates about full inclusion of LGBTIQ+ Christians and was just as divisive. At the time all Jewish males were circumcised as a way of upholding the covenant God made with Abraham. It was a key marker of identity and is still an important ritual for most Jews. The debate amongst early Jesus followers (who were ethnically Jews) was whether non-Jews had to become Jews first to be part of the Jesus movement. Paul didn't think so, but others did. It was clearly a heated debate, and at one point Paul tells his opponents that if they are so convinced of the importance of circumcision, they might as well go all the way and "castrate themselves" (Gal. 5:12)!

Paul argues that circumcision does not matter and should not be required for non-Jewish converts. His argument is effectively that everyone is reconciled to God ("justified" is Paul's language) because of the faithfulness of Jesus and our belief in him, not in following the law. Paul doesn't reject the law as unimportant but just doesn't think it is what gives one salvation. So, he argues, why require someone who is already saved by faith to adhere to the Hebrew law?

When we as contemporary readers get to texts like Galatians, much of the debate can seem irrelevant because circumcision is no longer a hot topic for Christianity (mostly because Paul won the argument). The deeper theological issue Paul addresses, however, remains a significant topic for today's church: Are biblical commands normative or prescriptive? That is, if there is a command in the Bible to do, or not do, something, is it applicable for all times and circumstances? Paul's interpretation suggests biblical laws are not timeless or prescriptive. What is most shocking in Galatians is that Paul sets aside a clear biblical command to circumcise all men as a sign of the covenant. Paul's interpretation of the Bible when it comes to circumcision challenges any interpretation that says Old Testament commands are always prescriptive for all people.

To apply the argument of Galatians to the contemporary church requires us to go to the heart, the kernel, of Paul's theology and leave aside the chaff that is the particular issue of circumcision. The pertinent question for the modern interpreter is whether or not one has to change part of who one is in order to become a Christian. Circumcision was the dividing line in Paul's time. In ours, the question of who is included and who is excluded, who is welcomed into faith and who is asked to change something about themselves, tends to manifest in matters of divorce, doctrinal commitments, sexuality, and gender diversity. As was the case for the matter of gentile circumcision, appeals to biblical commands loom large in these debates as we continue to tussle over whether certain commands should be read as normative and eternally prescriptive or can be set aside so as not to exclude people from the community of faith.

Nehemiah reminds us this contextual work is precisely the work we need to do for the Scriptures to continue to speak in our context. For Ezra and Nehemiah, this meant, amongst other things, changing Deuteronomic teaching on marriage to forbid marriage with *all* foreigners so that the Jewish community might reestablish itself in Judah (Ezra 9–10; Neh. 13).* This was applied retrospectively, and men were asked to divorce and send away their foreign wives and children, which they did.† For Paul the contextual work meant reevaluating the teaching in Genesis that all males in God's covenant community be circumcised and reinterpreting the Pentateuch to do so. In both cases the new teaching would have been controversial and shocking for many. Yet at the heart of both these radical reinterpretations of tradition is an attitude toward the Scriptures that is dynamic and flexible. It acknowledges the Bible is a living text through which God continues to speak in ways that address new communities and new contexts.

2 Peter: Correct and Incorrect Interpretation

The need to interpret "correctly" becomes an important issue in the New Testament as Christians begin interpreting the Old Testament to make sense of Jesus's life, death, and resurrection. How one interpreted the prophecies about the Messiah was paramount for making the case for Jesus. Again we see a range of factors associated with correct interpretation, including an emphasis on the role of community, the effect upon community, and the work of the Holy Spirit.

In Peter's second letter to Christians, he addresses the need to interpret every prophecy of the Bible, writing that "no prophecy of Scripture is a matter of one's own interpretation

* Deuteronomy 7:3–4 doesn't forbid intermarriage generally, but does list seven specific nations whom Israelites may not marry. Moses, Judah, and Joseph all married foreign women, and Ruth, a Moabite, is lauded for her faithfulness.

† We might note that while Nehemiah shows great inclusivity in terms of gender, there is an exclusivity in terms of ethnicity.

because no prophecy was produced by human will but rather men and women borne by the Holy Spirit spoke from God" (2 Pet. 1:20–21).* Peter here is primarily arguing for the reliability of the Old Testament prophetic texts because the prophets spoke through the Holy Spirit and so are inspired.† But he also stresses the need for correct interpretation of the prophets, warning his community that there are false prophets and false teachers. As he does later in reference to Paul's letters (3:16),‡ Peter acknowledges that interpretation can be wrong.

While we cannot build a model of interpretation solely from one text, and while that is not our intention, there are a couple of things of interest for us in 2 Peter as we think about interpretation. First, Peter acknowledges the need to interpret the prophetic texts of the Bible. We should note that for Jews, Moses the lawgiver was the greatest of prophets, so it is likely here that Peter refers to interpretation of all the Hebrew Bible, not just the parts we call prophecy. Second, Peter acknowledges that people who interpret the Scriptures can be wrong. How he determines this is less clear. Third, he uses the plural when he writes about those who interpret, implicitly acknowledging that this is a shared activity in the community, not something just one person or one leader does. Even when talking about himself as an eyewitness, he uses "we," confirming that he is part

---

* I am calling the author "Peter" for simplicity and because issues of authorship do not affect the point here. The majority of scholars recognize that 2 Peter is a later text strongly connected with Jude and therefore is probably too late to have been written by the historical apostle Peter. The author's name is best understood as a pseudonym drawing on the Petrine tradition.

The word translated as "interpretation" here is *epilusis*. It does not occur anywhere else in the New Testament but is found in noncanonical Christian and Jewish texts to refer to interpretation of prophetic dreams and visions.

† Jörg Frey, *The Letter of Jude and Second Letter of Peter: A Theological Commentary* (Waco, TX: Baylor University Press, 2018), 309–10.

‡ See pp. 36–37.

of a larger group who testifies to Jesus. Moreover, he is very clear that private prophetic interpretation is not to be trusted. Prophesying and reading and interpreting Scripture is a community activity. Lastly, while Peter doesn't tell us how or on what terms he would determine what is a true or false interpretation, he gives us one clue by writing that the false teachers "act secretly" and bring in "destruction" (2:1). In other words, good interpretation builds up rather than destroys, and is always open or transparent. This might be a good litmus test for any modern interpretation too.

Bringing Out the Meaning

One of the words scholars use to refer to interpretation is exegesis. The word from which we derive *exegesis* is the Greek verb *exēgeomai*, which literally means to "bring out" the meaning of the text, that is, to explain or interpret. Another term that means something similar is *hermēneuō*, from which we get the word *hermeneutics*. This also has the sense of explain, interpret, or translate. The New Testament uses these terms several times, and one of the consistent threads is that one can only "exegete," or explain, what one knows intimately.

Exegete is the word Luke uses when two of the disciples encounter the resurrected Jesus on the Emmaus Road and later explain (*exēgeomai*) their encounter with Jesus to the other disciples (24:35). These two men had spent the afternoon with Jesus prior to the meal, discussing the events surrounding Jesus's death and trying to make sense of it. Jesus had opened the Scriptures and interpreted them for the men (24:27). In shared conversation with one another, they begin to pull the threads together. When the presence of the risen Jesus becomes clear to them in the symbol of broken bread, they recognize that they had "burning hearts" the entire time Jesus was speaking. I sometimes wonder if this is close to what we might call a gut feeling, a sense of excitement for something even when you cannot yet articulate it. In this Luke 24 story, understanding Jesus's death has come about through discussion in community, significant time spent in conversation, explanation of the Old Testament, the addition of rituals, and divine help. It is then shared with others.

In John 1:18, Jesus is presented as the exegete or interpreter of God (*exēgeomai*), usually translated "made him known." John states that no one has seen God, and so we need someone to bridge that gap and make God known. Theologically in John's Gospel, Jesus is the one who points to God and makes God manifest in the flesh. Key to Jesus's ability to do this is his own closeness with God, which John describes in intimate terms. Jesus is "the one who was on the breast of the father"—a posture of great intimacy and affection. Only somebody that close to God can exegete or explain God. In the introduction, I wrote about the intimacy needed in wrestling like Jacob with God. Here we have another image of intimacy that hints at how we engage Scriptures: we need to know them. Not just our favorite bits of memorized proof texts. Not just the New Testament. We need a deep intimacy with the whole Bible if we are going to explain it to others.

We see a similar kind of intimacy in the explanations of Paul and the other apostles in Acts who explain the wonderful deeds happening among gentile converts to Christianity (Acts 10:8; 15:12–14; 21:19). That is, they share what they know, what they have experienced and seen for themselves. To bring out the meaning of something for others, be it a text or an event, requires us to have made sense of it ourselves. Every preacher knows that a sermon will fall short if we have not done the work of figuring out what a biblical passage means for us before trying to preach to others. Interpreting the Bible demands more than intellect or knowing a few things about language or history. It demands attention, intimacy, wrestling, and community, but most of all it requires a connection between reader and text.

If you think of the most meaningful events in your life, they are usually the ones charged with emotion and where there was deep connection with someone or something else. Whether it's a first kiss, your wedding day, the birth of a child, the death of a loved one, or a major personal achievement, the meaning of an event comes from the depth of connection between yourself and something outside yourself. Biblical interpretation can function in a similar way: meaning is made in the interaction, in the willingness to be vulnerable and the openness to be changed.

Conclusion

We began this chapter by noting that the Bible assumes that interpretation of the Bible is necessary for each new generation and context. We have discussed why we need to interpret the Bible and some of the factors that make that a complicated task for us in the twenty-first century. The difference in language and culture as well as the nature of ancient texts for which we cannot question the authors about their intentions means attention to history, linguistics, cultural difference, and a good dose of humility is needed. We have also touched on the various ways the Bible itself refers to biblical interpretation and have begun to see some themes emerge: an awareness that interpretation can be wrong, the role of community in faithful interpretation of Scripture, the need for time and study to develop an intimacy with the text, and the necessity of divine help. We have also noted that good interpretation of Scripture is something that builds up community.

In the next chapter, we will look at the nature of stories in the Bible, beginning with stories that exist in multiple versions or offer different perspectives on the same topic. Our question will be, What do we do when the Bible speaks in multiple and different ways about an issue?

CHAPTER THREE

Stories That Invite Conversation

They told the whole story of what had happened
to the demoniacs. Then the whole town came
out to meet Jesus.

— MATTHEW 8:33–34

Being selective in how you tell a story is not the same as being untruthful. I could tell you the story of my childhood in a number of ways. On the one hand, I had a wonderful childhood with two loving parents, siblings I mostly got along with (who doesn't fight with siblings?), a nice home, lots of friends, and extended family in the neighborhood. My childhood best friend, Lisa, and I walked from primary school most days through leafy suburban streets, playing games on the way and reveling in our seven-year-old freedom. At church on Sundays, I'd sing praise songs with my hands in the air, mimicking the adults, and romp with other kids after Sunday school. On summer days, I would go to a cousin's house to swim in their pool or one of our parents would take us all to the beach after school. We would pile into a station wagon, four or five across the back seat and more sitting in the trunk as the cousins headed to one of Cape Town's gorgeous white-sand beaches. Memories of childhood are marked by sunshine, laughter, sand, love, and licking passion fruit ice creams with great speed as I raced the sun's heat to catch the drips.

On the other hand, I could tell you the story of my childhood as one marked by fear, violence, and division. School was strict and challenges to authority were met with a cane or a paddle. As an easily distracted seven-year-old, I was caned for talking in class when absolute silence was required and paddled for forgetting my homework. It was a violence that reflected society at large and trained us for unquestioning obedience. My childhood world was rigidly ordered according to race: signs stated "whites only" or "colored car" to let you know which part of the train you were allowed on. Under an apartheid regime, our identity cards categorized us as "black," "colored," or "white" and had to be carried at all times. "Whites only" signs labeled public restrooms and were posted along those Cape Town beaches my family frequented. I could tell you too about the fear I saw in the eyes of the only Black people I knew—the housekeeper and gardener, who came once a week and treated us kids with a kindness we did not deserve. I could speak of the townships only a couple of kilometers from our suburban homes where kids I never met lived in corrugated iron shacks without running water, or I could recount the awkward, deafening silence at family gatherings when someone dared mention something to do with race or apartheid. I could tell you too of the horror my aunt expressed when I, as a young adult, drove into one of those shanty towns to take a Black man home. How had a white woman driven into a Black township and come out alive? she wondered. The fear was on both sides.

Both of these stories would be true and accurate versions of my childhood in South Africa. But the nature of my telling would depend on circumstance and the kind of connections I was trying to make. It would depend on my audience, my context, my purpose.

The ancient authors of the Bible are not so different. They told mythical stories, funny stories, sad stories, war stories, origin stories, prophetic stories, healing stories, stories that explain why thing are the way they are (etiologies), and stories about people's experiences of God. These stories were told differently depending on audience, time, place, and what issues they were addressing. Some of these stories differ from one another in their theological views of God, some give different perspectives about the same events, and some stories even contradict one another. We will begin by looking at stories that are told in different ways before moving to stories that seem to conflict with one another or diverge in their views. Finally, we will ask, How do we navigate divergent stories? How do we find God's voice amidst the differences?

STORIES WITH MULTIPLE VERSIONS: CREATION

Almost every culture has a mythical story about the origins of humanity and the world. These creation stories do a range of things—they explain why things are the way they are, why there is suffering or evil in the world, why humans behave the way they do, and what our relationship with God and the earth is like. In many Australian Indigenous cultures, for example, the creative deity is depicted as a Rainbow Serpent who creates and sustains life by bringing water to the waterholes but is also capable of whipping up a storm and punishing the people. Ancient Jews similarly recounted creation stories that addressed these kinds of questions, and we find several of them in the Bible. These mythical stories are clustered at the beginning of the Bible. The Bible does not just contain one creation story, it contains several. And sometimes they appear to contradict one another.

Genesis 2–3

When we open the Bible to read Genesis, we find the first three chapters are about creation. But this is not one story. Scholars agree that Genesis 2–3 was written first and Genesis 1 contains a different story that was added later, so I am going to address them in that order.

In Genesis 2:4–3:24 we find the famous story of Adam and Eve, the first humans. This creation myth* begins with a dry and

---

* I use the term *myth* to denote a mythical genre, that is a genre of dusty landscape where no plants grow because "God had not yet caused it to rain" (2:5). Dryness, drought, or lack of rain is a threat to life, and so God causing rain is part of God's life-giving gift. After causing water to come forth from the ground, the very first thing God creates is an *adam* from the dirt of the ground. The Hebrew here has a lovely play on words that gets lost in English. The word for earth in Hebrew is *adamah*, so the creature God makes from the dirt is an *adam*, literally an "earthling." The earthling becomes a living human being when God breathes into it the "breath of life" (2:7). We will return to humans in a moment, but the story takes us to gardens and animals next.

In this version of creation, God is like a farmer-gardener, planting a garden that will feed the *adam*, including some magical trees—the Tree of Life and the Tree of Knowledge of Good and Evil. Both of these are highly significant because the two main things this creation story does is explain why humans are mortal (have a limited lifespan) and why there is evil in the world. Both concepts relate directly to the trees. The *adam*/earthling is told not to eat from the Tree of Good and Evil, but he can eat from the Tree of Life at this stage, which will keep him alive indefinitely in this paradise garden.

The garden in which God places Adam is walled and has a river. Scholars think this concept of the garden reflects the ideal royal garden associated with Persian kings: places filled with exotic plants and delicious fruits that were protected from the outside world. Animals are created, but there is no suitable helper for Adam. We noted earlier that *helper* is a term used for God in the Bible, so a helper is a partner, someone capable of contributing in a way that animals cannot. This leads to the creation of Eve from Adam's rib, although she is not named

---

stories that are foundational for cultures and speak deep truths about the nature of the world. Calling something a myth is not saying it is untrue, although I recognize the term can be used like this in popular culture.

until much later. Her name is also a play on words, as Eve means "living" (*khavāh*). That she is taken from Adam's body is a way of showing how deeply connected human beings are to one another compared with animals.

This story also introduces the presence of evil and ultimately gives an account of how humans went from living in an ideal, paradise-like place to struggling to farm and living with pain. Evil, or at least temptation to do evil, enters the story in the form of a talking serpent, another sign we are dealing with mythical symbols (ancient people did not think snakes actually spoke). This serpent persuades the humans to eat from the Tree of Knowledge of Good and Evil so they will know more. What results is the introduction of shame; they hide from God, aware of their nudity and their wrongdoing. Their punishment is to be banned from the paradise garden (3:24) and therefore lose their access to the Tree of Life. They will now be mortal and life will be harder: they will have to toil for food; childbirth becomes necessary for ongoing life; birthing new life will be painful; and humans and snakes will continue to dislike each other. While this mythical story began as a creation story, we see that the main point is to give an explanation for why life is hard, food is scarce, pain is felt, and people die.

Theologically, the story preserves God's goodness—God wanted humans to live in paradise with God forever—and places the blame for the human condition on the human desire to over-reach and be like God. In the Christian tradition, however, this particular creation story is often cited to support heterosexual marriage, the subordination of women, and certain concepts of sin. Mythical stories are wonderful precisely because they operate at multiple levels, so I do not want to reduce it to just one meaning. In its original setting, however, Genesis 2–3 functioned primarily as a way to explain why humans feel alienated from God and one another as well as why people die and babies are born. Once humans are removed from the Tree of Life and their source of immortality, they need to give birth to new humans to continue the human race. Despite the aspects of struggle and pain in the story it is also used as the foundation for hope—hope that we will one day return to Eden and live in peace with God and nature again. The last book of the Bible, the book of Revelation, views humanity's final resting place as a return to Eden (called "New Jerusalem"). This paradise garden-city has a Tree of Life just like Eden and is where God and the people again live in harmony (Rev. 21–22).

Genesis 1:1–2:4a

While Genesis 2 imaged the pre-creation world as a dry, dusty place, the Genesis 1 creation myth begins with too much water. The world is a watery, dark, formless place into which God puts order and shape (1:2). Too much water in the form of floods or raging seas was a threat to life in the ancient world, just as it is now. So God creates dry places, separating land from sea and waters below from waters above so that there are safe places for humans and animals to dwell. Another stark difference is that humans are created last in this account, not first, and they are created as diverse genders to reflect the image of God—"let *us* make humans in *our* image" (1:26).

The creation account we know as Genesis 1 comes from the Priestly tradition of biblical writers. Priestly texts reflect priestly concerns, like keeping the Sabbath and proper procedures for cultic rituals. They are also interested in clarity regarding what makes humans pure or impure, holy or profane, and therefore which things should be kept separate from one another. In the Priestly tradition, being impure is not bad or sinful; it is just a state you are in until you do things to become pure again.* While you are impure, however, you must keep separate from

---

* Burying a body will make you impure, yet the Torah commands Israelites to bury their dead. Being impure is not being sinful; it just requires a purification ritual for cleanliness (see Num. 19:13).

pure things. Categories are very important to Priestly writers. We see such concerns in the highly ordered nature of Genesis 1, with its division of lights or water, structure of seven days, repeated refrains, and emphasis on resting on the Sabbath because God rested on the seventh day and declared it holy (2:2–3).*

There is no account of human sin or alienation from God in this story. Indeed, creation is repeatedly called "good" and at the end "very good" (1:31). Humans are even entrusted with the earth and all that is in it to "lord over" (sometimes translated "have dominion") creation. Part of lording over something is caring for it like God. Theologically, this account of creation presents the world as good because God has declared it so and ordered it into night and day, land and sea, and so on. We should note that these dualities (night and day, land and sea, male and female) are not a statement of distinct categories but rather reflect the poetic style of the story. As Old Testament scholar John Collins points out, just because there is night and day does not mean there is not dusk and dawn, when the light and dark "are not so clearly distinguished."† Sea and land are separated by the in-between spaces of tidal plains. Male and female, likewise, can be read as two ends of a spectrum, not a rejection of gender variation.

Humans are also good and reflect the image of God in this story, but God is a bit different from the God presented in Genesis 2–3. God does not walk and talk with humans on earth. Rather, God speaks and God's Spirit moves in a more transcendent manner. This reflects the theological diversity we see in the biblical tradition, where God is imagined in a wide variety of ways.

While there is a lot of rich theology and symbolism in the poetry of Genesis 1, there is good evidence to suggest that this

---

* I'm suggesting here that the seven days are symbolic and not literal and that reading seven as symbolic is the "plain sense" of the passage when we consider its poetic genre and its emphasis on Sabbath.

† John J. Collins, *What Are Biblical Values? What the Bible Says on Key Ethical Issues* (New Haven, CT: Yale University Press, 2019), 62.

version of creation was mainly written to affirm the pattern of seven days and the importance of Sabbath. That is, the primary objective was not to make a statement about the science or timing of creation but to show that the idea of Sabbath, a day of rest on the seventh day, was built into the very fabric of existence by God, and so it is a sacred and God-ordained day. While Christians have done an awful lot of theologizing from Genesis 1, very little of it continues to emphasize a pattern of regular Sabbath rest. Other concerns dominate, perhaps to our detriment.

Other Creation Stories in the Bible

The book of Job, as well as the Psalms and Isaiah, contains a reference to other creation myths associated with the chaotic monsters Behemoth and Leviathan (Job 3:8; 40:15; 41:1).* Behemoth is the name given to a land creature, whereas Leviathan is a sea serpent. Both are monstrous and chaotic forces who are contained, tamed, or crushed by God in the biblical tradition.

We see here the influence of other ancient myths from outside the Bible, specifically the Babylonian story of creation preserved in the Enuma Elish. Like Genesis 1, the Enuma Elish imagines the beginning of the world as a watery chaotic place that God needs to put in order. Unlike Genesis, the water produces two gods, one male (Apsu) and one female (Tiamet), who birth more gods. As the younger generation grows, fighting and violence between the gods breaks out, leading to Tiamet being cut in two and half her body being used to make the sky.

In some biblical accounts, which have arguably been influenced by such traditions, God creates these monsters much like the gods made other gods in the Enuma Elish. For example, the author of Job writes, "Look at Behemoth which I made just as I [God] made you" (Job 40:15; see also Gen. 1:21; Ps. 148:7). These monstrous creatures are part of creation but need to be kept in

---

* Leviathan also appears in Psalm 74:14; 104:26; and Isaiah 27:1.

check so that their violence does not overwhelm. While not a dominant strand in the Bible, the idea of monsters who must be controlled by God but who still wield some chaotic power is yet another way the Bible makes sense of the world through creation myths.

What to Do with These Creation Stories?

For some readers, becoming aware of the conflicting details in the creation stories can be disturbing and uncomfortable. To read them literally or as if they were a scientific account means one will inevitably run into the issue that they contradict one another. The creation of the earth cannot have started with *both* a dry, dusty place *and* a watery, dark place. Were humans created first or only after the animals? Are they primarily good or primarily rebellious?

I do not personally consider these creation myths contradictory stories because I do not think we are supposed to read them as literal or scientifically factual accounts of the origins of the world. Rather, they show that ancient Jews had various understandings about the way God interacts with God's world. If we read each story on its own terms to try and discern what it communicates, we can see their distinct theological points of view and appreciate each one for what it offers in helping us understand the richness and depth of divine activity. In Genesis 1, creation is affirmed as good because God has organized everything into its intended place. Part of that divine ordering of all life involves the weekly pattern: the seventh day is holy and set aside for rest because God rested. Keeping Sabbath is a way of remembering that God is in control and that all life is sacred. In Genesis 2, the story aims to do something very different: to explain why there is evil and suffering in the world (issues not even considered in Gen. 1). The presence of evil and our sense of disconnection from God and one another is explained through a story of human rebellion and alienation from the paradise God intended. The tradition of chaotic monsters found in Job and the Psalms is a different way to account for evil and suffering, this time due to nonhuman created forces that are constantly battling with God.

Multiple versions of origin stories indicate that not only did ancient Jews embrace multiple creation-type myths in order to address different theological concerns, but that the people who compiled the Old Testament kept differing versions of them and even put some of them side by side. It is not that ancient Jews were too simple to notice that Genesis 1 and 2 differed in significant ways, but rather that they knew they each had a specific truth to tell. The differences are a gift, not a problem to be explained away.

Despite their differences, there are also a number of similarities in these divergent stories. At their heart, each of these accounts credits God as having an active role in creation and affirms that humans hold a special place in creation in terms of our relationship with God and our responsibilities to God and the world. Additionally, each of these stories reflects something about the world that helps explain it: why we feel pain in childbirth, why we fear drought or flood, why we feel alienated from God and one another, why we yearn for (re)connection, why suffering can feel arbitrary, why most of us don't like snakes, why creation can be so good and beautiful but harsh and difficult all at the same time. What they do not do is tell us the scientific method by which God created. Science, in our modern sense, was not the point.

CONFLICTING STORIES

The second type of story we will look at are stories that appear to contradict or conflict with one another over a topic or aspect of faith. The main question here is what do we do with these? What does it mean that there are conflicting traditions in the Bible? We will look at just two examples from the Old Testament.

Redemption for Enemies: Jonah vs. Nahum

Jonah and Nahum are two short books that are part of the twelve "minor" prophets of the Old Testament. Despite both being prophetic texts, they give us two very different perspectives about God's treatment of enemies. The enemy in this case is Nineveh, the capital of Assyria, the empire that destroyed the northern part of Israel in 722 BCE and either killed or deported the Jews living there.* This northern region never recovered.

The book called Nahum tells the story of the prophet Nahum, who received a vision with an oracle "concerning Nineveh" (1:1). Written in the aftermath of the destruction of the north, this oracle speaks of God's wrath, rage, and vengeance toward Nineveh and God's ongoing protection of Judah (the remaining southern kingdom). It promises that God is "against" Nineveh and will humiliate it (3:5–7). The language is vivid and thick with emotion, describing Assyria as cruel and deserving of punishment. No opportunity for repentance is offered to the Ninevites.

Jonah was written after Nahum and presents a different view regarding Nineveh. The prophet Jonah is called to go to Nineveh and preach repentance. In a rather comical portrayal of Jonah as the ultimate reluctant prophet, the book of Jonah tells us he tries to flee God's call, spends three days in the belly of a big fish, and is eventually spewed out to do what God wants. Jonah's reluctance makes sense when we know Nahum and the broader history of Israel. The people of Nineveh are both gentiles and destroyers of God's people. They do not deserve God's mercy!

* Judah, the southern part of Israel, survived for approximately another 135 years, until the Babylonians came along and destroyed them too, including the temple in Jerusalem.

Jewish prophets were probably used to their warnings going unheeded, but in a rather astonishing turn of events, the whole of Nineveh, from the king to the animals, repents by putting on sackcloth and fasting in response to Jonah's message from God (3:6–8). We are told they repented of their "evil ways" and their "violence." God's mind is changed and God does not punish them (3:10). When his prophetic warning works and the people of Nineveh repent and are forgiven, Jonah sulks. He accuses God of being too gracious, too slow to anger, too "ready to relent from punishing" (4:2). Jonah is angry that God is merciful. In fact, Jonah is so angry he wants to die. He does not want to be the prophet who helped save Israel's enemy.

Nineveh ended up being destroyed by the Babylonians about fifty years after they had destroyed Israel. Nahum's prophecy may be an interpretation of this very event as an act of God's punishment. God is presented as protector of his tribe and a seeker of vengeance for wronged people in Nahum. Knowing God will avenge such horror may have offered both comfort and a sense of justice to the survivors. By contrast, Jonah presents God as profoundly merciful and forgiving, even of the worst enemies. By presenting such a radically different view, Jonah "invites us to interrogate our sense of justice" while theologically affirming God's radical graciousness.*

Nahum presents God as hating Nineveh and Jonah presents God as offering them compassion and loving-kindness. We may want to know which it is. Does God hate our enemies or love them? We might want a God who is clearly on *our* side (whichever side that is) and who feels the same way we do, but Nahum and Jonah challenge such a simplistic view. That both Jonah and Nahum exist side by side in the Bible means we are invited into

---

* Amy-Jill Levine and Marc Zvi Brettler, *The Bible with and without Jesus: How Jews and Christians Read the Same Stories Differently* (New York: HarperCollins, 2020), 316.

their conversation to explore our understandings of justice and divine mercy. We are invited to notice that even within one faith community there can be differing perspectives about what justice might look like. Like Jonah, we are called to have our expectations challenged by God's expansive graciousness.

Can I Have a Foreign Wife?

Whether Jewish men could or should marry foreign women is a matter of some debate in the Bible. On the one hand, we have texts that explicitly forbid marriage to a foreigner and, on the other, we have stories of faithful heroes who have foreign wives, as well as foreign wives who serve as exemplars of faith. If marriage to someone outside one's cultural or ethnic group was still a hot topic in modern western Christianity, we would find it hard to find one clear biblical teaching on the matter.

Ezra and Nehemiah are the most explicit in seeing foreigners as a threat. As the community tried to reform and regather after exile in Babylon, these leaders not only forbade marriage to non-Jewish women but also asked the men to send their foreign wives away. Amazingly, they did, at least according to the official record (Ezra 9:1–10:17; Neh. 13:23–31). In his speech to the people explaining why they had to send away their foreign wives, Ezra claims that the people "break [their] commandments again and intermarry" (9:14). The strange thing is the laws about marriage to a foreign woman are contradictory. On the one hand, Deuteronomy 7:3 prohibits men from marrying any women they meet when they enter the promised land out of fear these women will lead them to worship other gods. On the other hand, Deuteronomy 21 specifically allows that men going to war can marry the female captives, who would be foreigners. It states that they must treat such women as proper wives and not slaves, therefore granting them equal status under the law (Deut. 21:11–14).

Ezra goes so far as to name specific neighboring tribes that one cannot marry—Canaanites, Hittites, Jebusites, Moabites, and so on

(9:1). Yet the biblical story of Ruth identifies her as a Moabite numerous times. As a Moabite woman, Ruth is lauded for her faithful commitment to her family and to their faith (see Ruth 1:4). Ruth is highly aware of her status as a foreigner and shows surprise that Boaz, an upright Jewish man, would even take notice of her as a Moabite woman (Ruth 2:10). Boaz's response conveys the opposite of Ezra's teaching. He proclaims that Ruth's loyalty to her mother-in-law and her dead husband's people is deserving of God's reward and favor. Boaz eventually marries Ruth and they have children. King David is their great-grandson.* In other words, the greatest king in Jewish memory has a Moabite great-grandmother and it does not seem to be a problem for anyone. Indeed, Matthew's genealogy of Jesus's royal line includes several foreign women who are explicitly named as mothers (Matt. 1:2–16).

These diverse voices on the matter of marrying foreign women reflect diverse contexts and ideas. In Numbers 12, Aaron and Miriam express concerns that Moses has married a Cushite woman, revealing that marriage to outsiders was a source of concern throughout several periods of Jewish history. In the postexilic period, redeeming the identity of the Jewish people was paramount for Ezra and Nehemiah, who saw that removing foreigners and foreign influence would help protect the identity of the people. But other parts of Scripture show a greater openness and an acknowledgment that gentile foreigners are also capable of being faithful to God and are called to do God's work.

The question for us is, What do we do with such traditions? If we were to take Ezra-Nehemiah as normative or prescriptive, we might argue that Christians married to non-Christians should be compelled to send away their spouses and children since the main concern for these authors is not ethnicity but religion. Then, however, we would face a dilemma about divorce: Would this contravene Jesus's teaching that divorce is only permitted on the grounds of adultery (Matt. 19)? Alternatively, we can

* See Matthew 1:5–6.

read such stories as *descriptive* historical narratives rather than *prescriptive* commands. That is, to acknowledge that Ezra and Nehemiah were not writing prescriptive eternal commands that would govern every time and place going forward, but rather address a particular situation.

Not everything described in the Bible is good or there for us to imitate (think of all the accounts of rape, murder, war, lying, and adultery), yet so often Christians read the Bible as normative, as if the fact that something is in the Bible means it must be imitated. That is not the case. Ezra-Nehemiah give us insight into the kinds of concerns that governed a post-exilic community. For readers today, this ancient text invites larger questions, such as, Where are the limits to inclusion? What does God require of us? How do we cultivate a clear identity that will bring people together? How do we create community? These kinds of questions invite harder yet deeper reflection for any contemporary Christian community. It is not a matter of simply rejecting marriage to someone outside our religious or ethnic group. They may lead us to set some limits about inclusion and to think carefully about what we value most, but those limits and values may not be expressed in the same way as they were for Ezra. That is precisely the interpretive work we need to do when we read and interpret these biblical stories.

Conclusion

This chapter began with a quote from Matthew 8 about the power of telling a story. When Jesus heals two men possessed by demons, the men go and tell the entire town what has happened. As a result of their testimony, the entire town comes to meet Jesus. Stories are powerful, and stories about our experiences with God can be especially powerful. They can also be challenging. In the healing story I've just mentioned, the town ends up begging

Jesus to leave their region (Matt. 8:34). His presence and the change he embodies are too confronting.

In this chapter we have observed that the Bible contains versions of certain stories or a variety of perspectives on certain issues. We have also noted that the compilers of the Bible tend to have a generous policy of inclusion in that they do not exclude texts that contradict one another but leave them together as texts that speak about God in different ways. These observations can be unsettling in that they challenge any simplistic notion of unity ("the Bible says") and underscore the need for careful interpretation that considers both the finer details of any single text in its context as well as the larger story. This is not to say there is no unity in Scripture, but rather that we need to recognize where the unity lies and where there is diversity. We will return to the unity issue in a later chapter.

If you are like me, this is a challenge. I like things to be neat. I like things in categories. I want to know which version is true or correct. But the Bible does not behave like that. It invites us into an ancient conversation about God and God's people written over centuries, *and* it invites us into conversation with one another and our tradition as we wrestle with these texts. Nahum invites us to consider whom we count as enemies and why we desire vengeance. Jonah challenges our notions of justice with God's expansive mercy. And the prophets show us that God's people adopted different ethical principles at different times, depending on circumstance and context.

These observations can be challenging, but they are also liberating. They affirm that a diversity of experiences, theologies, and perspectives are woven into the very fabric of the Bible. For Christians who have been told their difference excludes them from the community or who feel constricted by a particular interpretation of what it means to be a "real Christian," knowing that God's community has always included a variety of people, perspectives, and experiences can be helpful.

In the next chapter we will look at an aspect of interpretation that we have not yet discussed—rewritten Scripture. Rewritten Scripture is the tradition of retelling or rewriting a story that already exists somewhere else in the Bible. What might surprise us is that as much as 50 percent of the Bible is "rewritten," that is, stories that are based on previous accounts and retold for new communities. This rewriting is an act of adaptation and ultimately interpretation.

CHAPTER FOUR

Scripture Rewriting Scripture

The biblical writers feel free to disagree with their
predecessors about how God's will and word to Israel are to be interpreted. But there is no disagreement
about the fact that God has spoken to Israel, and that
Israel consequently has an obligation to try and ren-
der that divine word "in human language" . . . as a
comprehensible guide for faith and life.

— ELLEN F. DAVIS
"Critical Traditioning"

The framers of the [Bible] kept interpreting and reinterpreting in order to make new texts.

— WALTER BRUEGGEMANN and TOD LINAFELT
An Introduction to the Old Testament

Fan fiction is alive and well. A quick search for Jane Austen–inspired spin-off novels, such as *What Kitty Did Next* or *The Jane Austen Book Club*, suggests well over forty such titles exist.* They are usually written by fans who do not want the story to end.

We tend to think of books as closed, contained, and finished things, but they are not. Books live afterlives in their readers' imaginations; they inspire spin-offs and sequels or are adapted into movies, either by the original author or a fan. Early Christians also wrote fan fiction. In the centuries following the New Testament, early Christians continued to write gospels, letters, apocalypses, and fictional stories based on biblical versions. In one of these, Paul converts a woman called Thecla, who becomes so enraptured by the gospel that she leaves her fiancé, breaks into prison to visit Paul, and later baptizes herself in a vat of seals whilst facing death (Acts of Paul and Thecla). The seals should have killed her, but by divine intervention lightning strikes and kills them before they can. It is a ripping tale about the power of the gospel to change lives and the bravery of Thecla as she faces martyrdom for her new faith. Other writings offer extensive

* A quick google search led me to discover there are far more of these than I had thought—over forty listed on one site that are all either spin-offs that continue the story where Jane Austen left it or retellings from a different character's point of view. https://the-bibliofile.com/jane-aus ten-inspired-books-and-retellings/.

tours of heaven and hell, extending the ideas found in Luke 16 and Revelation 19–22 in an effort to warn and persuade believers to remain moral (Apocalypse of Peter). We also have gospels that imagine another life of Jesus or present him offering different teachings (Gospel of Peter, Gospel of Thomas).

Prior to Christianity there was also a tradition of extending the biblical tradition, although it differs slightly from the afore-mentioned fan fiction tradition that extends stories. Numerous Jewish texts exist that effectively rewrite the Bible, many of which are in the Dead Sea Scrolls. Dating to the period between the Old and New Testaments (roughly the second century BCE to the first century CE), the Dead Sea Scrolls contain rewritten versions of Genesis, Exodus, and other biblical books. Some of the more well-known examples are Jubilees, Temple Scroll, and Genesis Apocryphon. In their rewriting of biblical books, the authors of these texts used a range of techniques to add new material, omit existing material, rearrange material, paraphrase, or adapt the language.* In many cases the editing and rewriting was done to strengthen or create connections between different biblical texts to show how the Bible speaks with a coherent voice or to clarify or update the text for a new context.†

These rewritings are not meant to mock or undermine Scripture—quite the opposite! They are a way of continuing the tradition and acknowledging the authority and importance of the subject matter. Similar to the way a modern preacher might illuminate a biblical text by appealing to a modern analogy or anecdote, these ancient Bible rewriters are evidence that "the faithful transmitter of the ancient and sacred tradition could, at the same time, be an innovator, whose own faithfulness to

* Molly M. Zahn, *Rethinking Rewritten Scripture: Composition and Exegesis in the 4QReworked Pentateuch Manuscripts* (Leiden: Brill, 2011), 14–15.

† Zahn, *Rethinking Rewritten Scripture*, 73, 231–34.

that textual tradition demanded the reshaping of it."* What is interesting is that this tradition of rewriting the Bible begins in the Bible itself.

Rewritten History

Anyone who has read through the Old Testament in order might have noticed it can seem repetitive. That's because it is. In the Old Testament, 1 and 2 Chronicles follow 1 and 2 Samuel and 1 and 2 Kings. The problem is that 1 and 2 Chronicles is telling the same story of the Israelite monarchy, so by the time you get to it, it feels like a hard slog (not helped by the fact that it starts with several chapters of really long genealogies).†

The Samuel and Kings narratives tell the story of the first king, Saul, through to the destruction of Judah and Babylonian exile about five hundred years later. At the point at which the narrative begins, God has functioned as Israel's king and order has been established through the help of prophets and judges. But the people demand a king "like other nations" (1 Sam. 8:5), something both God and the prophet Samuel warn them against. Samuel warns them that a king will take their sons for his army, their daughters as cooks and perfumers at the palace, and demand a portion of their produce (1 Sam. 8:10), but the people will not listen. It is a classic case of be careful what you wish for.

Writing after the exile to Babylon, the authors of 1–2 Samuel and 1–2 Kings are concerned to show why it seemed like God had abandoned Israel to a foreign power. How did they end up in exile? How did it all go so wrong? The Samuel and Kings texts propose that while some kings were good, many of them were bad

* Zahn, *Rethinking Rewritten Scripture*, 242.
† In the Jewish Bible, Chronicles comes at the end rather than straight after Kings, which we will see makes far more sense because it is a later retelling of the same events.

and led the people into idolatry and other behaviors that took them away from God. King Manasseh, for example, was remembered as one of the worst. As king, he was involved in making idols, practicing wizardry, making his son walk through fire, and filling Jerusalem with so much "innocent blood" that God became angry because of his evil (2 Kings 21; cf. 23:26). Such stories help to explain why things went so wrong.

Where Samuel and Kings tell a narrative of decline that explains why Israel ended up defeated and in exile,* Chronicles tells a story of the great monarch David to encourage hope in a future messianic king like him. This expectation, by the way, is why Jesus is called "son of David" in the gospels and why Matthew emphasizes that Jesus belongs to the royal line of David. Scholars believe that Chronicles was written much later than Samuel and Kings, probably several generations after the people had returned from exile. Hence, the concerns differed: Was God still with them? Were they still God's chosen people? How could Israel retain their greatness? Themes of repentance and the chance for forgiveness emerge as central, as does a very positive, idealized memory of King David as Israel's great king.

> Rewritten stories are texts that use other biblical texts as their source and retell an existing story. Note I am using the term *story* loosely here to denote a range of texts because the rewritten sections of the Bible include narratives, gospels, letters, poems, and law codes. Rewriting, as opposed to word-for-word copying, is its own kind of interpretation. In rewriting any tale, details might be added or omitted, emphases shifted, and arrangement altered as stories are retold for a new time, place, or audience.

* Gary N. Knoppers, "Treasures Won and Lost: Royal (Mis)appropriations in Kings and Chronicles," in *The Chronicler as Author: Studies in Text and Textures*, ed. M. Patrick Graham and Steven L. McKenzie (Sheffield, UK: Sheffield Academic Press, 1999), 181–208, 194.

In telling the story of King David, Chronicles makes several changes to the original Samuel-Kings account.* First, instead of David's kingship being contested as it is in 1 Samuel 31, Chronicles omits reference to Saul's surviving fourth son and presents David's elevation to the throne as unchallenged (1 Chron. 10–11). In Chronicles, David is appointed king because Saul's whole household has died and Saul has been "unfaithful," whereas David is both hero of the story and a paradigmatic king. Second, Chronicles makes David look better by portraying him as a highly successful military leader and famously omitting the story of King David and Bathsheba—the one where David spies her bathing from his high palace and summons her to his chambers to have sex with her. That David saw and took what he wanted was exactly the kind of thing the prophet Samuel warned the people a king would do. His actions contravene many Jewish laws, but it is her status as another man's wife that becomes a problem for David. When Bathsheba becomes pregnant, David tries to cover his tracks by ordering Uriah, her husband, to be killed. Murder and rape are not flattering behaviors for a king remembered as one of the great kings of Israel, so Chronicles leaves it out.†

In rewriting the history of Israel's monarchy, Chronicles is engaging in scriptural interpretation. The rewritten story is edited and shaped to offer hope to the people that God's promise of a future Davidic king who would reign forever was still true (see 2 Sam. 7). If we try to ignore or iron out the differences between Samuel, Kings, and Chronicles, we miss the message of the chronicler. This author is not just rewriting history for history's sake, but looking to the past to speak into a new context

---

* At times Chronicles also repeated Samuel almost word for word. Compare 1 Chronicles 10:1–14 and 1 Samuel 31:1–13.

† Chronicles also adds flattering stories about David that credit him with planning the temple if not building it. See 1 Chronicles 15–16; 22–29.

and give hope for the future: hope in a messianic king who will fulfill God's promise to David that "your throne will be established forever" (2 Sam. 7:16). We will see that the authors of the New Testament do the same thing.

REWRITTEN LAWS

It is not just the historical narratives of the Bible that contain rewritten versions of earlier accounts; it happens in the law-code sections too. If you are like me, you might glaze over when it comes to reading biblical laws and be tempted to skip this bit. But hang in there. In graduate school I had to take a class on Deuteronomy and I dreaded it. At the time, it was literally the last book of the Bible for which I would have chosen to do an in-depth exegetical class. But what I learned in that class blew my mind. Deuteronomy was radical, innovative, and responsible for so much core Jewish theology that one cannot imagine Judaism, or later Christianity, without it.

The law codes of the Bible are found predominantly in Exodus, Leviticus, and Deuteronomy. If you were to read through these books in order, you would find many of the laws are repeated in each. Indeed, Deuteronomy—whose title, *deuteronomos*, literally means "second law"—does not hide the fact that it is a retelling. Deuteronomy presents itself as a retrospective speech of Moses recounting the giving of the law in the past. It is therefore another classic example of Scripture retelling, or rewriting, an existing tradition.

Scholars generally agree that the laws of Exodus are the oldest legal strand and that the writers of Deuteronomy and the Priestly parts of Leviticus used Exodus as a base for their law codes, which were written down later. There is less agreement about the intention of these later writers: some scholars think that they intended to replace the previous laws with their versions,* while others think they intended to continue the Mosaic tradition, giving it new authority for a new generation.† The part I find most interesting is that the editors who put the ancient version of the Old Testament together kept them all. They chose not to give later readers only one version of Moses receiving the law, but rather left them all in there together, building diverse perspectives and variation into the Scriptures.

Case Study 1: The Ten Commandments

One obvious example of these multiple voices is the collection of laws known as the Decalogue or Ten Commandments, which forms the basis of the covenant God makes with the people through Moses. The Bible contains several versions of these.‡ The first account is in Exodus 20, where Moses, having come down from Mount Sinai, reads the words of the commandments to the people. The people are still in the desert at this point, having fled slavery in Egypt, and are yet to have reached the promised land. After the commandments are smashed in response to the people building an idol of a golden calf (Exod. 32), they are re-given in Exodus 34 as a sign of the covenant reinstated. Exodus claims that all editions of the tablets with the Ten Commandments were "written with the finger of God" and contained the "writing of God" (Exod. 31:18; 32:16; 34:1), giving them a unique status within the Bible.

Deuteronomy retells the giving of the Ten Commandments in the past tense as Moses reminds the people of the covenant God

---

* Jeffrey Stackert, *Rewriting the Torah: Literary Revision in Deuteronomy and the Holiness Legislation* (Tübingen: Mohr Siebeck, 2007), 211–12.

† Hindy Najman, *Seconding Sinai: The Development of Mosaic Discourse in Second Temple Judaism* (Leiden: Brill, 2003), 19–29.

‡ Exodus 20:1–17; 34:28; Deuteronomy 4:13; 5:1–21; 10:4.

made with them almost forty years earlier (5:1–21; 10:1–5). While the laws are almost verbatim, there are a few details that change.* Not insignificantly, in retelling the giving of the law, Moses charges the people that even though this was done in the past, it has ongoing relevance. He tells the people, "not with our ancestors did the LORD make this covenant, but with us, all of us here alive today" (5:3), effectively affirming the commandments' ongoing authority for God's people even a generation later. Taken literally, Deuteronomy 5:3 is not true: God made the first covenant with their ancestors, not with the later generation whom Moses addresses in Deuteronomy. Yet retelling and updating is a way of affirming authority and relevance for a new generation of God's people, and we might read Moses's speech to the people as the kind of rhetoric a preacher uses to say, "Listen up, this is speaking to you."

Case Study 2: Passover

Retelling a story can be a way to bring different traditions together or to replace earlier traditions. A classic example of this is found in the Passover instructions. Exodus 12 is the first Passover account, and the people are told to eat the lamb "roasted over fire" (12:8). The text is explicit not to eat it raw or "boiled [*bshl*] in water" (12:9). In Deuteronomy 16:7, however, the instructions are to boil (*bshl*) the lamb, directly contravening Exodus. Boil or roast—which is it? Ancient Jews noticed these contradictory instructions for Passover, and the later writers of Chronicles attempted to harmonize the two laws, writing, "they boiled [*bshl*] the Passover lamb with fire according to the custom" (2 Chron. 35:13).† That was not actually the custom, but Chronicles is trying to harmonize two different traditions.

---

* For example, "remember" the Sabbath (Exod. 20:8) as opposed to "observe" the sabbath (Deut. 5:12).

† Many English translations have also tried to even out the transla-

If the only difference between Deuteronomy and Exodus was boiling versus roasting, we might dismiss this as an insignificant change. Deuteronomy, however, makes numerous other changes to Passover. Instead of being a family festival celebrated in the home, Deuteronomy declares that it is not permitted to sacrifice the Passover lamb in any towns (16:5), but only in "the place" where God's name will dwell (16:6)—a reference to Jerusalem and the Jerusalem temple. Passover is also connected with the Festival of Unleavened Bread for the first time (16:3, 8), conflating what were two separate traditions into one longer festival. Scholars such as Bernard Levinson have argued this is part of Deuteronomy's larger agenda to centralize all cultic activities in Jerusalem,* a story narrated as part of King Josiah's reforms in 2 Kings 22–23.

Passover is not the only tradition Deuteronomy transforms. The centralization of the cult had implications for political and judicial life. For example, the law provided for someone who had killed another person without prior intent (manslaughter) to seek asylum at an altar to avoid retributive killing (Exod. 21:12–14). In Deuteronomy, this is transformed into a law that one can seek asylum in one of three designated towns (Deut. 19:1–13). This change is necessary precisely because Deuteronomy has banned all local altars and only permits one central altar in the Jerusalem temple. Hence the laws for asylum had to be updated accordingly.

In reshaping many of the laws found in Exodus, the writers of Deuteronomy simultaneously appeal to the authority of Moses and the Mosaic law *and* attempt to replace it with an updated one based upon cultic innovation. The irony, and gift to later generations, is that the compilers of the Bible put them side by side so

tion of 2 Chronicles, changing "boil" to "roast" even though the Hebrew term for roast differs.

* Bernard M. Levinson, *Deuteronomy and the Hermeneutics of Legal Innovation* (Oxford: Oxford University Press, 1998), 54–93.

we could see how one tradition interpreted and updated another for a new time and place. Updating the law was a way of giving it ongoing relevance and authority in the changed circumstance of a temple in Jerusalem and a centralized cultic system.

Case Study 3: Forgiveness

John's Gospel records a story of Jesus healing a man born blind (John 9:1–12). When the disciples first become aware of the man, they ask Jesus, "Who sinned, this man or his parents?" For modern readers it is a strange question. What does the sin of parents have to do with a child who was born without sight? But the disciples know their Torah and particularly Exodus.

There are several instances where the laws recorded in Exodus conflict with those in Deuteronomy even though both are attributed to Moses and both claim to be given from God. One example is the conflicting decree about sin and forgiveness in Exodus 34:6–7 and Deuteronomy 7:9–10. In the Exodus account, God is conversing with Moses on Mount Sinai and declares that children will be held accountable for the sins of their parents for up to four generations. Here is the full verse:

> The Lord, a God merciful and gracious, slow to anger, and abounding in steadfast love for the thousandth generation, forgiving iniquity and transgression and sin, yet by no means clearing the guilty, *but visiting the iniquity of the parents upon the children, and upon the children's children, to the third and fourth generation.* (Exod. 34:6–7)

The Deuteronomic version of this proclamation reads:

> Know therefore that the Lord your God is God, the faithful God who maintains covenant loyalty with those who love him and keep his commandments, to a thousand generations, *and who repays in their own person those who reject him.* He does

not delay but repays in their own person those who reject him. (Deut. 7:9–10)

Both of these texts affirm the loyalty and faithfulness of God toward God's people. Both also frame the outstanding extent of God's graciousness as something that will last for a thousand generations, a biblical way of saying an impossibly long time. The Deuteronomist, however, has changed the second part pertaining to punishment. Instead of children being held responsible for the sins of their parents as they are in Exodus, Deuteronomy holds the person who sinned responsible and no one else. Deuteronomy is both written later and presented as a speech of Moses with the benefit of hindsight. This new context perhaps prompted a theological update as the community looked back at the number of times God forgave them and continued to be faithful to them despite the frequency of their mistakes in the forty years of desert wandering.*

What do we do with such seemingly contradicting statements? The theologian Telford Work rejects the idea that these are contradictions and argues they are "sensitive reworkings of the text" consistent with the experience of Moses and the people that God does indeed forgive.† He claims we can see the development of theology in the biblical tradition as the people became more aware of the nature of God. I get nervous about the idea of "development" Work relies upon, which assumes humanity is on a linear trajectory of improvement. Where I do agree with Work is that within the pages of the Bible we have other parts of the Bible interpreting, updating, and adapting previous

---

* These ideas about God being slow to anger and generous in mercy are also found in later texts, such as Joel 2:12–14 and Jonah 3:8–10, which go even further than Deuteronomy in expressing God's radical willingness to forgive anyone who repents, including God's enemies.

† Telford Work, *Living and Active: Scripture in the Economy of Salvation* (Grand Rapids: Eerdmans, 2002), 150.

versions based on the later community's experiences of God. As noted in the previous chapter, the compilers of the Bible left all of these traditions together. Why? We can only speculate that perhaps they were more comfortable with a range of views than those of us enculturated by enlightenment thinking and its empiricism. Or they considered them all equally inspired by God and did not want to censure the divine. I think of these rewritten, diverse stories as a kind of testimony to the ongoing, dynamic relationship between God and God's people.* They bear witness to a people engaging their traditions and using them to continue a conversation with God in new times and places. Ancient biblical writers assumed that their sacred texts were speaking to each new generation and felt free to update them to address new circumstances and situations. The scriptural tradition served the community. It was not held rigidly in the past, but was a conduit for God to speak anew.

REWRITTEN GOSPELS

These rewritten parts of the Bible do not just occur in the Old Testament. Have you ever wondered why we have four gospels, four versions of the same basic story of Jesus's life, death, and resurrection? Matthew, Mark, Luke, and John all tell the same Jesus story, yet anyone who has read them carefully knows there are also some key differences. Only Matthew and Luke contain stories of Jesus's birth, and even then they tell it differently: Matthew gives us Joseph's perspective, complete with visits from

---

* I use the term "relationship" quite deliberately as an analogy: any good human relationship grows and changes in response to the needs and experiences of those involved. While some consistency of character and affection is necessary to sustain a relationship, one that never changes is usually problematic.

foreign magi and Herod's threat to kill Jesus, whereas Luke gives us Mary's song of praise, shepherds, and angels. We also get differences in the order of events, stories which are found in all four, and things which are found only in two or three, like the Lord's Prayer (which is only in Matt. 6:9–13 and Luke 11:2–4).

Scholars agree that Mark was the earliest of the gospels.* They disagree about how the other gospels relate to Mark, but the simplest explanation for the overlapping material is that Matthew knew and rewrote Mark, and Luke had both Mark and Matthew in front of him when he wrote his gospel.† After all, Luke tells us that he knows there are other gospels but he decided to write his own "orderly account" after "careful investigation" (Luke 1:1–3). Luke seemed to think there was room for improvement! Luke, like Matthew, also clearly had other information to include because it is only in Luke we find famous stories Jesus told, such as the Good Samaritan (Luke 10:25–37) and the Prodigal Son (15:11–24), or the account of Mary and Martha (10:38–42), or Jesus's appearance to some followers on the Emmaus Road (ch. 24).

In many ways these "Synoptic" (*synopsis* means "common view" or "seeing together") Gospels are the clearest example of rewriting in the Bible because there are parts that are word for word the same in Greek, showing literary dependence. One place we can clearly see this is in the baptism of Jesus. Matthew follows Mark almost word for word in places but then adds an explanatory note (in italics below):‡

---

* Matthew is first in the New Testament because for a while church leaders thought Matthew was the oldest and Mark had abbreviated him. There is now textual evidence that suggests the opposite.

† This is known as the Farrer hypothesis. It negates the need for a common source, traditionally referred to as Q (Quelle), to explain the common material between Matthew and Luke.

‡ Translations of the two passages are my own to show in English where the Greek matches or differs.

Mark 1:9–10	*Matthew 3:13–16*
In those days Jesus came from Nazareth of Galilee and he was baptized in the Jordan by John.	Then Jesus came from Galilee to John at the Jordan to be baptized by him. *But John prevented him saying, "I need to be baptized by you but you come to me?" And Jesus said to him, "Let it be, for it is proper to fulfill all righteousness." Then he consented.*
And immediately coming up from the water, he saw the heavens opened and the spirit descending, like a dove, upon him.	And when Jesus had been baptized, coming up from the water he saw the heavens opened, and he saw the spirit of God descending, like a dove, upon him.

In the context of Mark 1, John has been baptizing people with a "baptism of repentance for the forgiveness of sins" (1:4). A careful reader might ask, Why is Jesus baptized for repentance for sin unless he has sinned? The Christian church maintains Jesus was sinless, so what is going on here? Matthew seems concerned with precisely this dilemma, so he makes sure to clarify it by including a dialogue between Jesus and John on precisely this question.

John's Gospel is the most different from the others at a number of levels. There is a reasonable amount of debate about how it relates to Matthew, Mark, and Luke, and we don't really know if this author was "rewriting" the other gospels or simply doing his own thing based on some common traditions. John still tells the same general story of Jesus's life, death, and resurrection, but it begins with a statement about Jesus's being the eternal word (*logos*) who entered the world as "the word became flesh" (1:14) rather than a birth story. John also has a different chronology. Instead of going up to Jerusalem only once in his lifetime, Jesus goes to Jerusalem several times as a faithful Jewish man might. Much of the change in arrangement or chronology serves a theological purpose for John. For example, John uniquely says Jesus died on the eve of the Passover (not the Passover day as in the other gospels), which is when the Passover lamb would traditionally have been sacrificed. This fits with his theology that Jesus is the "lamb of God" who will liberate and save his people from God's judgment like the Passover lamb (1:29).

When we look at the differences between the four gospels, and there are many, we can clearly see that they are theologically motivated. These authors were not interested in writing a historically precise account of events for the sake of history alone. They were not impartial (not that any history is impartial). They were writing about "good news" (*euangelion*), and they wanted their readers to know that Jesus was God's son, the promised Messiah, and that his death and resurrection could save them. They were writing theology. Or to put it another way, they were testifying to something that had changed their lives and, like any testimony, getting across the experience of what God had done in Jesus was far more important than whether some particular thing happened at three p.m. on Tuesday or seven p.m. on Sunday.

One place we can see how each gospel writer theologically shapes their testimony is in the words that Jesus says on the cross. It is possible Jesus said all or none of these things, and it is hard to know who might have been close enough to hear. The gospel writers have, however, shaped Jesus's final words to fit their theological portrait of him. Starting with Mark, Jesus says the following on the cross:

Mark:	My God, my God, why have you forsaken me? (Mark 15:34)
Matthew:	My God, my God, why have you forsaken me? (Matt. 27:46)
Luke:	Father forgive them, for they do not know what they are doing. (Luke 23:34)
	Truly I tell you, today you will be with me in paradise. (Luke 23:43)
	Father, into your hands I commend my spirit. (Luke 23:46)

John: Woman, here is your son. . . . Here is your mother.
          (John 19:26–27)
          I am thirsty. (John 19:28)
          It is accomplished. (John 19:30)

In Mark, all the disciples flee and desert Jesus in his final hours. Mark's portrayal of Jesus's death is of a man who suffers the most horrendous pain—not just physical pain, but the spiritual and psychological pain of feeling abandoned by everyone, including God. It is a portrait of the ultimate suffering for the sake of humanity. Matthew follows Mark closely but adds other events to Jesus's death, including apocalyptic earthquakes and rising dead people to show that Jesus's death shakes the very fabric of the cosmos (Matt. 27:51–53). Luke does something a bit different. He emphasizes the innocence of Jesus and the role of forgiveness in his gospel. In Luke, Jesus forgives others and promises them paradise. He dies calmly, giving over his spirit to God, trusting that God will vindicate his unjust death (which God does in the resurrection). In Luke's crucifixion scene, the centurion declares, "surely this man was innocent" and omits "this is God's son," which occurs in Matthew and Mark. In doing so, Luke has rewritten, reshaped, and omitted material from the other gospels, then added his own words or sources to emphasize that Jesus's death is an injustice (23:47). Lastly, John is again different. For John, Jesus is in control and his death is the culmination of his purpose and life. He makes sure his mother is taken care of, he fulfills Scripture by asking for a drink, and then he "gives up his spirit" when ready. When he breathes his last in John, Jesus is breathing out his promised Spirit, for he has accomplished what he has come to do as the Passover lamb.

While the core event is the same, each of these crucifixion scenes emphasizes something different and something important about Jesus's death: he was innocent, his death was unjust, his suffering was extreme, he willingly submitted to the cross, he offered paradise to others, he placed himself in the hands of

God, and he cared for his own until the very end. To ask which is most true or historically accurate is to miss the deeper point these testimonies are making.

For some in the early church, four versions of the same "gospel" was a bit of an issue. Irenaeus, a second-century bishop, argued that the four gospels were the four pillars of the church and four were necessary. He appealed to the idea that there are four corners of the created earth and four living creatures in Ezekiel to justify why four were needed. In other words, he appealed to the Bible to argue that four is biblical and as God intended. Others tried to harmonize the four, suggesting that not everyone was comfortable with such diversity. Tatian, also a second-century Christian, created a gospel harmony known as the Diatessaron. It was a compilation of all four gospels into a single coherent narrative that could be read in church and would continue to be used for some time.

The point here is the gospels continue the tradition of the Bible rewriting the Bible that started in the Old Testament. In doing so, each gospel contributes a particular theological emphasis and, in some cases, new information and stories. We might think of these diverse and repeated stories in the Bible as being like a cut diamond. If we only ever view such a diamond from one angle, we might still notice how brilliant and pretty it is, but we might not be able to tell if we are looking at something round, oval, square, or rectangular. The way the Bible speaks about God is similar. To use the gospels as an example, if we only have Mark's Gospel, we would have one view of the diamond. Matthew, Luke, and John give us different perspectives. They all speak of the same God and tell the same central story about God's son, Jesus, but they each give us a slightly different angle on it. Together, we get a fuller sense of the God whom we seek to know and follow. Together, they offer us a broader description of the life of Jesus and a richer perspective of the meaning of his death and resurrection.

Rewritten Letters

The tradition of rewriting texts that had become authoritative, popular, or relevant to faith communities in some way (remembering that there was not yet an agreed canonical "Bible") continues in the New Testament beyond the four gospels. Readers of 2 Peter and Jude have long noticed how similar they are. In fact, 2 Peter is far more similar to Jude than it is to 1 Peter in terms of language, content, and style.

Second Peter and Jude both use similar language and refer to similar concepts in a similar order. Both begin with a greeting that includes language of "peace" and "abundance" (Jude 2; 2 Peter 1:2); both are concerned about false teachers who "sneak in" (Jude 4; 2 Peter 2:1); both talk about angels who sinned and have been kept in "chains" in "deepest darkness" until judgement day (Jude 6; 2 Peter 2:4); and both implore their readers, writing, "beloved . . . remember the words spoken beforehand by the apostles" (Jude 17–18; 2 Peter 3:1–3).* These parallels are strong enough to suggest one of the authors had a copy of the other letter or that he or she shared a common source.† Either way, we have two letters that share a similarity much like the Synoptic Gospels.

Conclusion

In this chapter we have seen that one of the ways the Bible interprets the Bible is to retell or rewrite the story for a new time and place. By my calculation, as much as 50 percent of the Bible

* For a full list, see Jeremy F. Hultin, "The Literary Relationship Among 1 Peter, 2 Peter, and Jude," in *Reading 1–2 Peter and Jude: A Resource for Students* (Atlanta: Society of Biblical Literature, 2014), 29–30.

† There has been much debate about whether Jude used 2 Peter or vice versa. Another option is that they shared a common source. Hultin, "The Literary Relationship among 1 Peter, 2 Peter, and Jude," 32–40.

is rewritten. The idea that rewriting the Bible can be a way to uphold its authority seems counterintuitive, but I would argue that this is precisely what happens. Rewriting the Bible affirms the Bible, keeping it alive and relevant for each new generation or changing context. These biblical accounts of rewriting the Bible model for us a way of interacting with God's Word that never just repeats it but is always interpreting it and engaging it for each new context. When we open the Bible, there is a sense that we get to listen in on a conversation between God's people, God, and their sacred texts as they continuously grapple with questions of faith and faithfulness. It is a conversation into which we are invited all these centuries later.

Christianity was birthed in stories: stories about Jesus's healing powers or battles with the demonic, stories Jesus told about the Kingdom of God, and, of course, stories about the resurrection. Indeed, without people sharing stories about their encounters with Jesus, there would be no Christianity. The gospels are full of such stories, and much of the preaching we overhear the apostles doing in Acts is their sharing their stories, their testimonies, about Jesus. These stories drew people to Jesus, people who wanted to know more, wanted to ask questions, wanted further conversation. In the next chapter we turn to the New Testament and begin by asking what kind of interpreter Jesus was when he preached and taught using his Bible, the Old Testament.

Jesus as Interpreter

And beginning from Moses and all the prophets,
Jesus interpreted for them all the Scriptures
concerning himself.

— LUKE 24:27

Several years ago, "what would Jesus do" (WWJD) wristbands and T-shirts were very popular in certain Christian circles. Wearing a WWJD wristband was a helpful reminder to check in, to pause, to reflect on whether one's behavior was in accordance with his. Even though I was part of those circles having earnest conversations about what Jesus might have done in any number of situations, we rarely talked about what Jesus would have done when it came to interpreting the Bible. How would Jesus interpret the Bible? How *did* Jesus interpret the Bible? Fortunately, we have numerous examples in the New Testament of Jesus reading, proclaiming, and unpacking the Scriptures.

In the contemporary world, liberal Christians tend to want to make Jesus inclusive and loving on all occasions. Jesus the "nice guy" is attractive and easy to sell. Conservative Christians point to a Jesus who isn't afraid to proclaim judgment and teaches the highest moral standards. The truth is, inconveniently, somewhere in between. Jesus defies our neat modern categories. At times the gospels show that Jesus is radically inclusive and merciful in ways that challenge traditional interpretations of Scripture and Jewish identity. At other times, Jesus is the conservative one, upholding Torah, proclaiming judgment, and calling his audience to return to a deeper and more demanding allegiance to the Scriptures compared with some other Jewish teachers at the time. His teaching provoked strong reactions from his audience, ranging from love, obedience, and awe to fear, hatred, and anger.

Amidst this complexity, a picture emerges of a Jesus who was considered an authoritative teacher of the Bible, someone who frequently appealed to the Scriptures in his teaching and who assumed the Scriptures speak to the present with authority and relevance. Jesus as interpreter, we shall see, is a Jesus who prioritizes people, mercy, and compassion.

As I discussed in the previous chapter, Jesus's words come to us through the authors of the four gospels. When scholars talk about Jesus interpreting Scripture, they usually talk about Mark's or Luke's use of Scripture, attributing the nuance of any interpretation of the Old Testament to the authors of the gospels.* There is good reason for this: we do not have a separate record of Jesus's exact words but only what the authors of the gospels have recorded, and these authors have each shaped the Jesus stories into their particular theological narrative. That is not to say they are not true or there is no historical veracity for Jesus's words in the gospels. Rather, it is to remind ourselves that no one followed Jesus around with a tape recorder or notebook, and so the words of Jesus, even Jesus as interpreter of his Bible, are mediated through the gospel authors. For the sake of simplicity, however, I am going to talk about Jesus as interpreter (rather than "Jesus in Luke," for example). While I want to acknowledge that the portrait of Jesus takes on a particular and unique shape in each of the four gospels, I think we can find common threads in the ways Jesus uses and interprets Scripture in all four gospels.

Our goal in this chapter is to unpack some of the ways Jesus interpreted his Bible (the Old Testament) to see if there is a model in his method of interpretation that we contemporary Christians might follow or learn from. What I propose is that Jesus uses Scripture to talk about who he is and about how

---

* See for example the detailed study of Richard B. Hays, *Echoes of Scripture in the Gospels* (Waco, TX: Baylor University Press, 2016).

to treat others. We shall also see that Jesus is primarily "anti-fundamentalist" in the way he uses Scripture.* He freely combines different Old Testament passages to make a new point, he claims Scripture has been fulfilled in himself, and he argues about how to interpret *torah* (law).

SCRIPTURE AND JESUS'S IDENTITY

The first thing to note as we discuss Jesus's use of the Bible is that Jesus assumed Scripture was authoritative and holy. His teaching was in keeping with the Jewish tradition, and he quoted both the Torah (Pentateuch) and the prophets as if they had ongoing relevance and authority for his audiences—because they did. In what follows we will look at the way Jesus interpreted *torah* (instruction/law) like other Jewish leaders and how he interpreted the prophetic texts of the Bible in reference to himself and his identity. We will take examples from each of the four gospels, although these are by no means exhaustive and much more could be said. We begin with identity.

Jesus as Interpreter of Himself in Luke

In Luke's Gospel, there are three key moments where Jesus uses the Scriptures to point to his identity. The first occurs at the beginning of Jesus's ministry in Luke 4. Jesus is in the synagogue and opens the Isaiah scroll like a scribe would. He proceeds to read this passage:

> "The Spirit of the Lord is upon me,
>   because he has anointed me

* William Loader, *Jesus and the Fundamentalism of His Day* (Grand Rapids: Eerdmans, 2001), 140.

> to bring good news to the poor.
> He has sent me to proclaim release to the captives
> and recovery of sight to the blind,
> to let the oppressed go free,
> to proclaim the year of the Lord's favor."
>
> (Luke 4:18–19)

When he is finished, Jesus sits and says, "Today this scripture has been fulfilled in your hearing." In doing so Jesus claims that he is the Spirit-anointed figure prophesied in Isaiah who will liberate Israel and bring good news to the poor. He confidently asserts that the promises God gave to Isaiah hundreds of years earlier have ongoing relevance. As we saw in our earlier discussion of the way the prophets use other Old Testament passages, Jesus likewise treats Scripture as a living, dynamic way of interacting with God. It is not something that just belongs in the past. He places himself in the prophecy of Isaiah and then effectively says, "this is happening right now. I am part of God's plan."

The actual quote Jesus reads is a combination of Isaiah 61:1–2 and 58:6. It breaks off right before the part about vengeance in Isaiah 61:2 and includes a section of 58:6—"let the oppressed go free."* Whether Luke misremembers or Jesus (or Luke) deliberately combined two different sections to make a new point, we will never really know. The effect, though, is that Jesus's role as liberator or releaser of captives is emphasized. The Greek word for "release" (*aphesis*) is sometimes translated as "forgiveness" or "letting go." Jesus is one who releases both from unseen forces, like sin (release from which we might call forgiveness), and external forces that enslave or imprison people, like poverty, slavery, or systemic racism (signs of communal sinfulness). The various English translations of the word *aphesis* throughout the Bible reflect the

---

* Isaiah 61:2 in its entirety reads, "to proclaim the year of the LORD's favor, and the day of vengeance of our God; to comfort all who mourn."

context in which the word is used and also the theological views of those translating it. In Greek, though, the same word is used for both spiritual and physical release, suggesting a holistic view of the mercy and liberative grace offered by God in Jesus. God's liberating grace encompasses the physical and the spiritual, the political and the religious. Jesus embodies this fullness throughout his ministry, but it is a fullness that we in the modern church often fail to live out ourselves, which is why interpretation matters so much. Too often we prioritize one over the other, either praying for people but doing nothing to change their circumstances or being social justice warriors whose actions are divorced from prayer and worship. Getting this theological balance right is hard but essential, as release from both the spiritual and physical powers that bind us is a key part of Jesus's preaching and role.

We might also note that Jesus's claim in Luke 4 begins a conversation and evokes strong emotions. As Jesus and the other Jews in the synagogue continue discussing the passage he has just read, they ask him questions and he talks more about the way prophets get treated. As he goes deeper into the implications of what he is saying, the crowd turns from amazement to anger. They don't like his interpretation and want to hurl him off a cliff (Luke 4:29). For those of us in the contemporary church who sometimes get despondent about how emotional and awful debates about biblical interpretation can be, this is an important passage. There is perhaps comfort in knowing that even Jesus faced enormous criticism for his interpretation of the Bible. But there is also a warning here that when we react in anger or reject another's interpretation, we may well be behaving like the crowd in the story. We might be rejecting the words of the Holy Spirit. How can we maintain a posture of openness and humility in reading Scripture together, even when there are strong differences of opinion about the best interpretation?

The second instance of Jesus's acting explicitly as interpreter of the Scriptures in reference to himself occurs after his resurrection (Luke 24:13–35). Jesus appears to two disciples as they travel to Emmaus from Jerusalem, pondering the death of Jesus and the things they heard about him. They don't recognize Jesus and they speak to him as if to a stranger. This is one of the few passages in the New Testament that explicitly refers to Jesus interpreting Scripture (see the quote at the top of this chapter). We are not told much of what Jesus says, just that he "interpreted" or "explained" (*diermēneuō*) the Scriptures to them as they concerned himself. That is, Jesus unpacked the prophetic texts to show that he was the promised Messiah and that he had to die. Key to the message seems to be his explanation that the Messiah's suffering was already declared in the prophets. This is probably because Jesus's suffering and death would have been the most controversial part of his life and a likely barrier to people believing he was the Messiah. In explaining the prophets, Jesus is showing how his life *and* death are consistent with the way the Old Testament spoke about the Messiah to come.

The Emmaus Road story is infused with many supernatural elements and high emotion: the men's eyes are kept from recognizing Jesus, their hearts "burn" as he speaks with them, and Jesus vanishes as rapidly and miraculously as he first appeared. Ultimately these two disciples come to recognize him in the combination of the interpretation of Scripture and the sharing of a eucharistic meal. Together, ritual, biblical interpretation, and community lead to the disclosure of the full reality of God in Christ.

An interesting element of the exchange in Luke 24 is that most of the talking is done by the two men who tell Jesus about "the events" that have happened in Jerusalem. They share their experiences, and Jesus helps them to connect it with Scripture. Help is needed because such connections are not actually obvious. The Lukan scholar John Carroll writes, "These texts do not offer self-evident connections to Jesus's role and ministry, for he must interpret (*diermēneuein*, v. 27) them in such a way that the connections can be discerned and hidden meanings opened up (*dianoigein*, vv. 32, 45) so as to be seen and understood."* Jesus as interpreter here is someone who engages people where they are, who listens to their experiences, and who helps them connect that experience with the Scriptures. It's a people-centered approach and one that again assumes Scripture has something relevant to say to each situation. Scripture is treated as something that can add meaning and fullness to human experience and struggle.

Similarly, in the third example, Jesus interprets the Scriptures for a larger group of disciples. In this penultimate scene in Luke's Gospel, Jesus appears to the disciples, who are gathered in a locked room (24:36–49). They are startled by his appearance even though he greets them with peace and shows them his wounds so they know it is really him. This is the first time they have seen him since his death and reported resurrection, so there is a combination of joy and disbelief. After eating with them, he again "opens up" (*dianoigein*) their minds to understand the Scriptures. Luke says he interprets the law of Moses (Torah), the prophets, and the Psalms—which is a way of referring to the entire Old Testament. Again, we don't know precisely which passages he unpacked, but he sums up in the following way: "thus it is written, the Messiah must suffer and will rise on the third day" (24:46). He goes on to talk about repentance, evangelism, and the disciples' role as witnesses to him. This time, the unpacking of Scripture is not just so they understand but also because they are tasked with the mission of testifying to "all nations." The "opening up" of minds toward Scripture leads to an opening out in mission toward others. It is expansive. When Jesus interprets, not only does he open up individual hearts and minds but he encourages those who hear to open themselves to others.

These later Lukan passages offer a striking model for the contemporary pastor, leader, or biblical teacher: Jesus begins with the experience and knowledge of others and then helps to make con-

* John T. Carroll, *Luke* (Louisville: Westminster John Knox, 2012), 485.

nections and draw out meaning until a moment of recognition is reached. Jesus assumes that the prophets need to be interpreted to be understood. Understanding occurs in conversation and in community. It involves an opening up to God, to one another, and to the Bible itself. But understanding is not for its own sake. Once those connections are made for the hearers, once they grasp who Jesus is, Jesus calls disciples to share the good news.

Jesus as the One Who Embodies God for John

John's Gospel records Jesus using Scripture in a slightly different way, although still to refer to himself and his identity. There are two things I would like to highlight here. First, Jesus in John often talks about himself in the third person to point to his relationship with God as God's Son. He also shows that his death on a cross is not only part of God's plan but consistent with God's past action. A classic example takes place in John 3 where Jesus is talking with Nicodemus, one of the Jewish teachers. Jesus compares himself with Moses, or more precisely with the bronze snake that Moses lifted up as a source of healing for all those bitten by poisonous snakes in the desert. You can read that story in Numbers 21:1–9. Jesus teaches that his death on the cross will operate in a similar way, offering life and healing to all those who look upon it with faith (John 3:14–16). By connecting the cross with an ancient story of how God saved the Israelites in the desert, Jesus reminds them that transforming an object of death into something that saves life is what God does.

Jesus repeats this type of biblical teaching in 5:21–27, again using Father and Son language to show that his death and resurrection are part of God's long-term plan for everyone to have life. He connects his activities with another part of the Exodus story—the account of God providing the people manna in the desert when they were hungry. This emphasis on life as God's gift and goal comes to the fore in John 6 when Jesus starts saying "I am . . .":

I am the bread of life. Whoever comes to me will never be hungry. (6:35)

I am the bread that came down from heaven. (6:41)

I am the bread of life. (6:48)

I am the living bread . . . I will give my life for the world. (6:51)

The words "life" and "living" are repeated numerous times in this passage as Jesus teaches that he brings eternal life whereas other bread only sustains life temporarily. By evoking a well-known passage of Scripture about the Israelites relying on God for manna in the desert to survive, Jesus uses Scripture to show that God has always fed the people, sustained their lives, and is continuing to do so in Jesus. Similarly, in John 10 Jesus appeals to a well-known image of a shepherd. A shepherd is another biblical image for a leader whom God tasks with caring for the people—a role Jesus now embodies perfectly. As Good Shepherd, Jesus says he calls his sheep and lays down his life for them. His mission is summarized as "I have come that they might have life and have it abundantly" (John 10:10). It might prompt us to ask if our mission, evangelism, and biblical interpretation bring abundant life to others.

We have only touched on a few brief examples from Luke and John that give us a glimpse into the way Jesus used Scripture, albeit through the lens of the gospel writers. In all of them, Jesus is depicted as emphasizing the consistency of God's character and of God's desire that all people have life. In Luke's Gospel, Jesus appeals to the words of the prophets and the authority of the Scriptures to point to himself. In John's Gospel, Jesus uses Bible stories more generally to appeal to the very nature of God as loving and life-giving. It is Jesus's closeness with God, as Son and one "from heaven," that means he embodies God and God's gifts in a unique way: he is the bread, he is the life, he is the truth, he is the Son, and his cross will be God's gift raised up for all to see.*

JESUS AND *TORAH* (INSTRUCTION/LAW)

In addition to quoting Scripture to point to his identity as Israel's promised Messiah, Jesus also interpreted commandments from the *torah*. In a manner typical of Judaism at the time, Jesus engaged in debates about what the various laws mean and how they should be best applied. He assumes *torah* is authoritative, but also that laws need interpretation to work out how best to apply them for a new time and place.

Attitude Matters, Not Just Behavior (Matthew)

Matthew's Gospel is the most explicit of the gospels in presenting Jesus as a teacher of *torah*, which is to say, an interpreter of *torah*. This can be seen most clearly in the Sermon on the Mount in Matthew 5–7, where Jesus unpacks six legal passages. This section opens with

The written Torah is the first five books of the Bible, what Christians call the Pentateuch. Written Torah includes narratives, promises, laws, commandments, creation stories, and Moses's prophecies, which are all foundational for Jewish faith. The term *torah* is a Hebrew word that means something like instruction, teaching, or law. Often we translate it as "law" in the Christian tradition, but this can give a sense that such teachings are very legalistic when they are better thought of as instruction for ethical living that goes beyond judicial matters and includes matters pertaining to worship, social justice, and relationships.

---

* Jesus also refers to himself as the way (14:6), gate (10:7–9), light (8:12), good shepherd (10:11), true vine (15:1–5), and resurrection (11:25) in John.

Jesus "teaching" his disciples (and perhaps a crowd) on a mountain. The mountain evokes the Moses tradition: Moses received the commandments from God on the mountain, and now Jesus will expound upon them while also on a mountain.

Jesus claims he is not there to abolish the law but to fulfill it. "Not a single stroke will pass away from the law," he proclaims (Matt. 5:18). Yet immediately he starts to challenge not the law itself, but some classic interpretations. When Jesus says, "You have heard it said . . . but I say to you," he is acknowledging existing Jewish interpretations of legal passages and then providing his own alternative. He does this for several traditional commandments pertaining to murder, adultery, divorce, making oaths, and retribution. Take the following example:

> You have heard that it was said, "You shall not commit adultery." But I say to you that everyone who looks at a woman with lust has already committed adultery with her in his heart. If your right eye causes you to sin, tear it out and throw it away; it is better for you to lose one of your members than for your whole body to be thrown into hell. And if your right hand causes you to sin, cut it off and throw it away; it is better for you to lose one of your members than for your whole body to go into hell. (Matt. 5:27–30)

What is Jesus doing here? He quotes the commandment "do not commit adultery," which is primarily about condemning the act of adultery. He then offers an interpretation that moves to the kinds of attitudes that would precede any act of adultery. The Greek here literally means "do not even look at another woman with lust." The audience here is presumed to be male and married—normative for most Jewish men over a certain age at that time. The biblical scholar Craig Keener points out that in a culture where women were held responsible for preventing lust by covering themselves up, Jesus tells men they are responsible for their thoughts and desires.* The image is graphic and dramatic: if you're a man who cannot stop looking with lust, don't blame the woman—tear out your own eyes! In other words, it's your problem, men, not the women's.

This is not a watering down of the *torah*. Neither is Jesus rejecting *torah*. Rather he is rejecting the interpretation of it given by the scribes and Pharisees and pointing out what they have missed. Jesus shifts the focus of the law from the outward behavior to the internal attitude, and in doing so, raises the moral standard.† Many married people manage to refrain from committing adultery during their marriages. But far fewer married people would be able to claim they haven't fantasized about someone else, cheated emotionally, flirted with someone they found attractive, or looked at another person with desire at some point. While it is a very good thing that one's partner does not act on attraction toward someone other than his or her spouse, Jesus points to a much more demanding ethic. He prioritizes love and respect for a spouse even when it comes to one's inner thoughts and attitudes. To not look with lust on another is a way of honoring one's partner and keeping one's attention, love, and desire focused on them exclusively. It is a much higher moral bar.

In a similar vein, "do not murder" becomes don't even hate another person to the extent that you would think about doing them harm. "Do not swear falsely" becomes, in Jesus's interpretation, don't swear an oath at all but be true to your word at all times. If you are always completely honest and act with integrity, there is no need to swear an oath because your "yes" means "yes" and your "no" means "no" (Matt. 5:37).‡ In both these cases

---

* Craig S. Keener, *The Gospel of Matthew: A Socio-Rhetorical Commentary* (Grand Rapids: Eerdmans, 2009), 187.

† Loader, *Jesus and the Fundamentalism of His Day*, 83–84.

‡ A sentiment repeated in James 5:12.

Jesus teaches that it is the underlying attitude and consistent integrity that matters to God, not simply the outward action. In doing so he points beyond the practicalities of the law to their intention—love and respect toward all people. In making these interpretive moves, Jesus actually increases the ethical demands of the law. The ultimate expression of this comes in 5:44: "love your enemies and pray for those who persecute you." Jesus extends the existing ethic of "love your neighbor" (from Lev. 19:18) to include those who do not treat you well. Followers of Jesus must not hate even enemies and those who seek to harm them. Jesus argues from a general theological principle rather than quoting a particular Scripture (because one does not exist for this particular teaching)—if God sends rain and sunshine alike on good and evil people, then who are we to distinguish? Imploring his followers to "be perfect" like God (5:48), Jesus demands they love like God.

Jesus teaches something very similar when he tells the story about a Good Samaritan (Luke 10:25–27). In response to a lawyer's question of "who is my neighbor?" Jesus tells a story about an outsider, a Samaritan, who shows mercy and care to a beaten man and therefore acts as his neighbor even though they come from different religious and geographic areas. It is worth noting that the question in Luke comes from a lawyer, that is, an interpreter of the Jewish *torah*, and so it is primarily a question about how to interpret the Scriptures and where the ethical obligations of *torah* lie. Indeed, anytime Jesus is asked a question about ethics by another Jew, he is really being asked to interpret the Scriptures. The teaching Jesus presents through the parable is the same as we find in Matthew—that the command to love extends beyond traditional kinfolk to those who might be considered strangers or even enemies.

We will look more closely at Jesus's emphasis on love for neighbor and enemies in the next chapter and delve more deeply into it there. For the author of Matthew's Gospel, love of God and neighbor is the key to interpreting all Scripture. Later Christians will follow him in this emphasis.

Laws Exist for People, Not People for Laws (Mark)

We live with laws every day, laws that are designed to keep us safe, like speed limits for drivers, mandatory seat belts, and prohibitions and punishments for murder, rape, or other crimes. These laws are not there for their own sake but are designed, ideally, to protect society and particularly the vulnerable. But no law is perfect, and all laws require interpretation and awareness of context if they are to be enforced in a fair way. Why else would we have so many lawyers, juries, and judges?* How one applies the law, even today, requires interpretation and consideration of circumstance and mitigating factors.

Imagine, for example, someone driving down the highway at one hundred miles per hour, well over the speed limit. What does the driver look like in your mind? If we visualize a drunk young man behaving irresponsibly after a night out at the pub with friends, we might well want the full weight of the law thrown at him for recklessly endangering his own and others' lives. But what if the driver is a different young man, a father-to-be, driving his pregnant wife to the hospital because she has gone into labor, no ambulances are available, and she is bleeding and screaming in pain? Would we want the full weight of punishments enforced or might we want leniency because he is acting in the service of another human being and possibly saving a life? These are the kinds of ethical dilemmas that Jesus and other Jewish leaders debated

---

* Laws, in our modern context, also get updated as attitudes in the community change. For example, marital rape became a crime in many countries only in the 1980s and 1990s as attitudes changed and society began to recognize that consent always matters, even in existing relationships. It was also once illegal to engage in homosexual sex. That is no longer the case in the majority of countries.

about: not about driving speeds, but about practical matters at the time, such as how to keep the Sabbath.

As well as increasing the ethical demands of the law to include attitudes, Jesus teaches that compassion and mercy toward others are key to interpreting *torah*. One of the areas where we see how Jesus prioritizes human need over commandments is in his interpretation of Sabbath commandments. Sabbath teachings can be found in numerous places in the Old Testament. The first Genesis creation account reaches its literary climax when God rests on the seventh day and declares it holy (Gen. 2:3). Keeping the Sabbath holy is one of the Ten Commandments (Exod. 20:8–11; Deut. 5:12–15) and it is upheld for animals as well as humans and even in the time of wandering in the desert and gathering manna to eat (Exod. 16:25–26). In the Old Testament the general rule is that no matter your circumstance, Jews and everyone in their households are to keep Sabbath as it is holy time. There were exceptions, though, particularly when it came to saving a life.

In Mark 2:23–3:6, we read two stories where Jesus and his disciples are accused of contravening Sabbath commands. It is hard to overemphasize how important keeping Sabbath was, and still is, for the identity and cultic life of Jewish people. So, when Jesus appears to break Sabbath, he is challenging some deeply held values and behaving in a way that is profoundly offensive to other Jews.

In the first account, Jesus and his disciples are plucking grain as they walk through the fields. It is Sabbath and presumably they are going to the synagogue to worship. Technically, plucking or harvesting is "work" and so is banned on the Sabbath along with food preparation and other forms of labor (Exod. 16:23–26; 20:10; Deut. 5:14). When the Pharisees ask why he allows his disciples to behave unlawfully on the Sabbath, Jesus's response is to argue by biblical analogy. He does not dispute that they are "working" but argues that since David and his friends could eat the bread put out as an offering for God, that is, holy bread, when "in need" and were not punished (1 Sam. 21), Jesus and his disciples can do so too. Matthew's version of this story makes it clearer that the disciples were eating the grain and that their actions were motivated by hunger like David's (12:1–8).*

Imagine a starving stranger walking into a church on a Sunday morning and taking the communion bread before the service has started. In most Christian traditions this would be considered a bit rude and in some highly offensive. Jesus argues that if someone is in need or hungry, that takes precedence over ritual, convention, and Sabbath norms. He is not denigrating keeping the Sabbath as a principle, but rather saying compassion for a human being comes first. As Matthew Thiessen puts it, "mercy takes precedence."†

The conversation could have ended there, but Jesus doubles down with more biblical interpretation. He evokes Genesis 1:26–31, where God creates the seventh day and declares it a holy day of rest, a "Sabbath." Jesus infers from this that God created Sabbath for humans (who were created on day six). That is, Sabbath is a gift of rest for God's people, not something to make their lives harder.‡

The second incident occurs when Jesus gets to the synagogue. He sees a man with a shriveled hand and heals him. Again, he is accused of breaking the Sabbath commands not to work because healing is considered work (Mark 3:1–6). There is legal resonance to the way Mark tells the story—Jesus is being watched by people who might "bring charges" against him, possibly the death sentence in accordance with Numbers 15:32–36 and Exodus 31:14–15. Jesus asks the crowd, "Is it permitted to do good on the Sabbath

---

* The scholarly consensus is that Matthew is written after Mark's gospel and the author of Matthew uses Mark as one of his sources. So Matthew makes more explicit what is implied in Mark's earlier account.

† Matthew Thiessen, *Jesus and the Forces of Death* (Grand Rapids: Baker Academic, 2020), 161.

‡ See Leviticus 16:31; 23:32.

or to do harm, to save life or to kill it?" The obvious answer is that it is not permitted to harm and kill but it is permitted to save a life. There is evidence that Jewish rabbis around this period argued one could and should contravene normal Sabbath rules in order to save a human life.* But the crowd is silent, and Jesus is grieved at their lack of compassion for the man.

To us, this man's disability does not appear to be life-threatening and Jesus seems to be making a rather large leap from "saving a life" to "doing good," which is not the same thing. Yet in the ancient world, where mortality rates were much higher and life spans shorter, any illness was closely associated with death.† It might be like one of us hearing the diagnosis of cancer from our doctor. When we hear the C-word, we immediately fear the worst because of the association between cancer and death. Statistically most cancer is treatable if not curable. In some cases, the survival rate is over 80 percent, but that doesn't mean a diagnosis won't strike fear into any of our hearts. Having a disability or illness in antiquity was much the same. It made one incredibly vulnerable.

Jesus's response to the man with a shriveled hand is to again argue that God is primarily concerned for people and thus laws are designed to help people live well. So, compassion trumps Sabbath. That is not a rejection of the commandments, but rather a way of taking them seriously.‡ For most modern Christians for whom keeping a strict Sabbath is no longer a big deal, Jesus's prioritizing of mercy and human need over Sabbath law may simply seem obvious, nice, or the easy option. That could not be further from the truth in his context. Mark records that

* Joel Marcus, *Mark 1–8* (New York: Doubleday, 2002), 248.

† Matthew Thiessen, *Jesus and the Forces of Death*, 167. Thiessen points out that while physical disability does not seem life-threatening from our modern medical view, the association with death could be attributed to demonic activity in the person or to the awareness that some disabilities shorten life.

‡ Loader, *Jesus and the Fundamentalism of His Day*, 18.

the reaction to Jesus's healing work on the Sabbath was a plot to kill him by those who had accused him of breaking Sabbath (Mark 3:6).* That is how offensive his behavior was to some of his kin. Yet Jesus underscores that people come first—"Sabbath was made for humans, not humans for the Sabbath" (Mark 2:27). Jesus's affirmation of human life over Sabbath reflects one strand of first-century Judaism, but a highly contested one.

Jesus's insistence that mercy and compassion toward people is the first priority in the application of the law was very costly for him. It can be similarly costly for many today. Those who have argued for the inclusion of women in ordained church ministry or affirmation of LGBTIQ+ Christians know too well the kind of hostile reaction one can get for giving precedence to mercy and compassion when interpreting Scripture. I have had colleagues and friends, pastors and academics, who have lost their jobs in their church or seminary because they changed their views or spoke up about their acceptance of LGBTIQ+ Christians or women's leadership. In some cases the hatred, harassment, and abuse they have received from Christians who were once their friends or colleagues has been astonishing. Yet compassion and mercy for people who are vulnerable or marginalized is the model of Jesus. This approach of Jesus, to put people before laws, would lead later Christians to set aside circumcision requirements and food laws in an effort to include more people in God's Kingdom (see Paul's letter to the Galatians).

Jesus's teaching and actions relating to Sabbath laws consistently emphasize that mercy and compassion toward a human being is more important than ritual or keeping law for law's sake. Mercy, compassion, healing, and feeding are acts of love. They are ways of loving the other and treating them as we would want

* Mark's masterful storytelling hints that, ironically, plotting or holding any kind of meeting relating to work was also prohibited on the Sabbath, so those who accuse Jesus of working go and do the same themselves.

to be treated if we were hungry, sick, or having a hard time. In this sense, Jesus's attitude toward the Sabbath in Mark's Gospel is entirely consistent with his emphasis on love in Matthew 5–7 when it comes to interpreting *torah*. While Sabbath keeping is not a major concern for the majority of Christians in the twenty-first century, the deeper principles of mercy, compassion, and love remain a key to interpreting Scripture in our own time.

Conclusion

"People too often assume that to interpret and reinterpret Scripture in light of changed realities or changed perceptions of reality is a modern phenomenon. It is not. It was a central issue in Jesus's disputes with his contemporaries and continued to be central to the church in New Testament times," writes William Loader.* In this chapter we have seen that Jesus engages in biblical interpretation and in disputes about interpretation with his contemporaries. He frequently argues with other Jewish leaders and scholars—scribes, Pharisees, and lawyers—about how best to interpret Scripture when it comes to applying the *torah* in his context. Although the ethical issues Jesus addresses differ greatly—ranging from murder to Sabbath keeping—Jesus consistently emphasizes love, mercy, and compassion for other people when it comes to interpreting *torah*.

We read Jesus's interpretation as it comes down to us in the pages of the Bible, which means we are interpreting Jesus's interpretation of the Bible. I am suggesting here that our goal is not to immediately apply Jesus's interpretation to our context in a literalistic way, but rather to interpret like he did, to mimic his approach rather than treat his conclusions as prescriptions for every context. This is a challenging and important point.

---

* Loader, *Jesus and the Fundamentalism of His Day*, 3.

Jesus's teachings include timeless truths, but they are also deeply contextual. As we have seen above, Jesus addresses specific situations within specific contexts. For example, Sabbath keeping is not a contentious issue for most Christians, but Jesus's teaching on the matter has application for other areas of contemporary life. In what ways do we put rules or tradition before people? Are we overlooking human need in the pursuit of perfect ritual or rigid application of the Bible? Have we failed to have compassion for someone who is different to us? Does our teaching bring life? The point is not for us to parrot Jesus's words or treat our favored interpretation as the only one possible, but to do the more demanding work of imitating his ethic of love and his attitude of mercy.

If we applied a WWJD ethic to biblical interpretation, we might consider the following ways we can read and interpret the Bible like Jesus did:

- foster a deep knowledge of the Old Testament so that its stories, ideas, and theology become part of our lives;
- approach the act of reading and interpreting Scripture with prayer;
- expect the Scriptures to speak—they are part of an ongoing, living conversation between God and God's people;
- cultivate an attitude of openness: openness to what new thing the Spirit is saying through the Scriptures rather than looking for confirmation of what we already know;
- expect to have to interpret: ask questions about your own agenda and context as well as the context of the words on the page to find the deeper meaning behind any given teaching;
- prioritize people over ritual or rules: we get caught up in getting church, doctrine, or praxis "right" and sometimes forget that it is all there to serve people;
- look to the Bible to help you love those who are different from you and even those who hate you;

- interpret with integrity: match internal attitudes and outward behavior;
- and act with compassion toward others.

In the next chapter we will discover that early Christians summed this all up under the command to love: love God, love neighbor. That is what Jesus did.

A Hermeneutic of Love

You shall love your neighbor as yourself.

— LEVITICUS 19:18

Jesus said to him, "You shall love the Lord your God with
all your heart, and all your soul, and all your mind. This is
the greatest and first commandment. And the second is like
it: You shall love your neighbor as yourself. On these two
commandments hang all the law and the prophets."

— MATTHEW 22:36–40

For the whole law is fulfilled in a single saying,
"You shall love your neighbor as yourself."

— GALATIANS 5:14

If you really fulfill the royal law according to Scripture,
"You shall love your neighbor as yourself," you do well.

— JAMES 2:8

A few years ago, I sat down over coffee in a fancy Melbourne hotel with the head of a conservative Christian lobby group. We were discussing Christian responses to various pieces of proposed government legislation related to gender and sexuality.* He explained to me that one of their projects was fighting for the rights of Christian parents and foster parents to be able to insist their children go through gay-conversion therapy.† When I asked him if he was worried about what such practices would do to the children given the evidence that they cause harm and that it didn't seem very loving, he seemed genuinely surprised.‡ "What is more loving than stopping someone going to hell?" he asked.

* At the time Australians were preparing to vote in a referendum about same-gender marriage, and several related bills, such as those regarding religious freedom, were being discussed.

† Note that while "therapy" is the traditional language, practices that aim to suppress or change someone's sexual orientation have been widely dismissed by licensed counselors and psychologists as effective or as therapy. Gay-conversion "practices" include any attempts to change someone's sexual orientation. Such practices range from prayer and counseling to cognitive training and electric shock therapy.

‡ Timothy W. Jones, Anna Brown, Lee Carnie, Gillian Fletcher, and William Leonard, *Preventing Harm, Promoting Justice: Responding to LGBT Conversion Therapy in Australia* (Melbourne: Gay and Lesbian Health Victoria, LaTrobe University, and the Human Rights Law Centre, 2018).

That conversation has stuck with me. We both thought we were following the gospel and loving our neighbor, but we disagreed about the best way to love. He thought he was being loving in trying to save people from the eternal damnation he believes awaits anyone who acts on same-gender attraction. I, however, have been convinced by the evidence from former leaders of gay-conversion practices and survivors that tell us that not only is there zero evidence anybody's sexuality can be changed but, moreover, attempting to do so leads to high rates of PTSD, suicide, and ongoing trauma for people who have gone through such programs or been exposed to these practices.* How can causing trauma to already vulnerable and often marginalized people be loving?

The disagreement between myself and my Christian brother in that hotel lobby was partly about love but mostly about biblical interpretation. We both agreed that following Jesus means living out our faith in tangible ways; we agreed that love involves action, but we disagreed about what kind of action because we disagreed about how to interpret the Bible.

So far in this book, we have journeyed with the Bible noting the many ways the various authors of the Bible have adapted, edited, rewritten, and variously interpreted earlier biblical texts in order to help the Bible "speak" in new contexts and situations. This indicates a dynamic, living biblical tradition—one that continuously puts the written word in relationship with the communities who consider these texts sacred or authoritative for the way they speak about God.

* Alan Chambers, the past president of the Christian organization Exodus International, whose mission was to help people suppress or change their homosexuality, has admitted such attempts do not work 99.9 percent of the time. He has apologized for the pain caused in trying to do so. Exodus International has now closed. See Alan Chambers, *My Exodus from Fear to Grace* (Grand Rapids: Zondervan, 2015).

Such dynamism within the Bible itself raises a set of questions about how best to interpret the Bible in the contemporary world. That is, it raises hermeneutical questions ("hermeneutics" meaning the theory and method of interpretation). Given the enormous flexibility within the Bible when it comes to interpreting the Bible, what is the best way to interpret? Does anything go? Can we discern a set of rules or guidelines from the Bible itself? How much can we update and contextualize biblical teaching, and how do we know when we have crossed a line and transformed it into something of our own making rather than God's?

A legitimate concern of those who advocate for a literal interpretation of Scripture is that if we make too many allowances for our modern cultural values, we are at risk of skewing Scripture to our own personal biases. We might go astray from God's truth. Such concerns can, however, lead to an unyielding allegiance to the "truth" of Scripture over all other forms of knowledge, particularly science, and lead some Christians to reject contemporary scientific insights about evolution, climate change, types of illnesses, gender, sexuality, and a range of other topics. While I am very sympathetic to the underlying concern to be faithful to Scripture, the solution offered by those advocating for a literalistic or fundamentalist reading is ironically one that tries to turn Scripture into something it never was: a science book, an idol, or a rule book that is fixed in time. It is a rejection of the living, breathing, Spirit-filled, and dynamic relationship between God's people and God that has been the thread holding what we call "the Bible" together. To cling to a fundamentalist view of the Bible is to ignore its very nature.

Others set limits on interpretation by giving priority to the historical or "original" meaning of the text.* Scholars like myself,

---

* *Original* is a problematic term, not least because we do not have the original copy of anything in the Bible, only copies of copies of copies (see ch. 1, p. 13). The appeal to the original is often framed as the original

who do academic and historical work on the Bible, can get a little obsessed with the historical or intended meaning of the Bible. Some argue that the intention of the original author(s) should always govern our own interpretations. Others put the emphasis on the interpretation of the first recipients as something that should govern our interpretation. While we can learn a lot by seeking to understand the historical context of both first authors and first readers, why privilege their interpretation over all others? We have seen that Jesus and others in the Bible routinely adapt and even update Scripture when applying it to new contexts and new issues, so the Bible itself testifies to a tradition of Scripture being interpreted and reinterpreted rather than giving precedence to the earliest interpretation. That is, the Bible itself models interpretation that moves beyond authorial intent. So the question is not whether we should interpret or even update interpretations, but how to do it faithfully. What ethical or theological principles might guide our interpretation?

What I propose in this chapter is that the earliest interpreters of Scripture—Jesus and the authors of the New Testament—did have an ethic that guided their interpretation. It is one that transcends any particular context or time and exemplifies the very nature of the God Christians worship. This ethic is love: love of God and love of neighbor. It is deceptively simple and surprisingly difficult to enact.

The Love Command

The Old Testament verse most quoted in the New Testament is Leviticus 19:18b—"you shall love your neighbor as yourself."

---

intention of the author or the interpretation of the first audiences who received these texts. Determining authorial intent or the interpretation of first communities is itself an act of theoretical, historical construction.

Sometimes called the "golden rule" or "love command," this ethic of mutual human love can be found in a variety of forms in different religions, but within the Old Testament it only appears in Leviticus 19. Despite its rarity in the Old Testament, the command to love is quoted by almost every New Testament writer, suggesting that in the centuries between Leviticus and Jesus, love of neighbor became especially important in Judaism. In the New Testament, the command to love neighbor is usually paired with the command to love God—"you shall love the LORD your God with all your heart, with all your soul, and all your strength" (Deut. 6:5)—to form what is referred to as the "double love" command: love God and love neighbor. This is the greatest command according to Jesus and his contemporaries (Matt. 22:37; Mark 12:31). How did the command to love become so central?

The Love Command in Judaism

The love command in Judaism occurs first in Leviticus. Leviticus is often perceived as a rather tedious book to read as it is full of commands that mostly feel archaic or irrelevant to modern life. It includes detailed instructions on how to make certain cultic sacrifices, farming instructions about inter-species animal breeding or leaving grain for gleaning, and several instructions about what constitutes acceptable sexual relations. If Christians know anything about Leviticus, it is usually the few verses pertaining to sexual activity. Yet, in the midst of numerous rules for various aspects of life (harvest, sacrifice, Sabbath keeping), comes the love command in two forms:

> You shall not hate in your heart anyone of your kin; you shall reprove your neighbor, or you will incur guilt against yourself. You shall not take vengeance or bear a grudge against any of your people, *but you shall love your neighbor as yourself.* I am YHWH. (19:17–18)

The stranger who resides with you in your land shall be to you
as the citizen among you; *you shall love the stranger as yourself*
for you were strangers in Egypt. (19:34)

"Love" (*ahab*) in Hebrew is a word that encompasses a whole
range of relationships, from God's love toward God's people, to
romantic love, to parent-child love, to neighborly obligations.
Love here is not simply a feeling, but neither is it a law in the
modern legal sense. These verses in Leviticus 19 are part of a section of Leviticus known as the Holiness Code (Lev. 17–26). They
function as wisdom or guidance for holy living. In its context,
the command to love is primarily about practical and ethical
behavior toward those in your community.

The command to love one's neighbor in Leviticus 19:18 is
introduced with a reminder first not to hate "anyone of your kin"
(Lev. 19:17). Kin language likely refers to fellow Israelites and
indicates that the primary focus is on one's obligation toward
fellow Jews.* Later, in Leviticus 19:34, the command to love is
extended to strangers or "aliens" who live in the land, widening
the scope of love beyond immediate kin or those of the same
ethnicity or religion (19:34). Leviticus, therefore, commands radical love in the midst of a set of other rules for holy living. Love
describes an ethical act: practical behavior based on loving treatment of those around you whether they be kin or strangers.

Love also appears in many other parts of the Old Testament. Most English translations of the Psalms have constant
refrains about the "steadfast love" of the Lord.† The Hebrew
word translated as "love" here is *khesed*, which means "loving-
kindness." It refers to God's behavior toward the people and is

---

* Kengo Akiyama, *The Love of Neighbour in Ancient Judaism: The Re-
ception of Leviticus 19:18 in the Hebrew Bible, the Septuagint, the Book of
Jubilees, the Dead Sea Scrolls, and the New Testament*, Ancient Judaism and
Early Christianity 105 (Boston: Brill, 2018), 23, 66.

† For example, see Psalms 5:7; 31:21; 40:10; and 136. There are over one
hundred verses proclaiming God's steadfast love (*khesed*) in the Psalms.

repeated throughout the Bible as a core attribute of the divine
and one that the people should imitate in their own acts of
loving-kindness.*

This command to love one's neighbor does not appear again
in the Old Testament yet is everywhere in the New Testament.
What happened in between? How and why did this one small
phrase become so prevalent in the New Testament period? Did
Jesus introduce a new emphasis? The answer to these questions is
not easy, but we do see a use and development of Leviticus 19:18
in other Jewish literature before and around the time of Jesus.

The book of Jubilees is one piece of the puzzle. Written in
Hebrew around 160–100 BCE, Jubilees is a retelling of Genesis 1
to Exodus 16 that emphasizes the Mosaic law and the holiness of
the Sabbath. While not considered canonical in most Christian
traditions, we know early Christians read Jubilees and quoted
from it. It is also evidence of the ways Jews were interpreting
Scripture (the Old Testament) and reflecting theologically in the
two hundred years between the end of the Old Testament and
the emergence of Jesus. Jubilees quotes Leviticus 19:18, writing it
into the Genesis narrative at several points. The love-command
is presented primarily as a way to keep family peace.

If we want to understand the kind of Jewish world that shaped
Jesus and his first followers, the collection of texts known as the
Dead Sea Scrolls (DSS) found in the caves of Qumran, Israel, is
key. The Dead Sea Scrolls are a collection of ancient Jewish scrolls
containing copies of the Bible as well as many other Jewish writings, such as hymns, prayers, and community guidelines. They
were discovered in the 1940s and have hugely increased our insight
into Judaism in the centuries prior to the New Testament. While
there are numerous texts in this collection that quote or allude to

* See 2 Chronicles 20:21: "Give thanks to the Lord, for his steadfast
love [*khesed*] endures forever." See also Nehemiah 9:17; 1 Chronicles 16:41;
Ezra 3:11; Job 10:12; Jeremiah 33:11; Lamentations 3:22; Daniel 9:4. Hosea
6:6 clearly states that loving-kindness is required of God's people too.

Leviticus 19:18, at least two DSS view it as central to their ethic.* The first is the Damascus Document (abbreviated as CD), which gives community rules and paraphrases Leviticus to do so: each man is to love his brother as himself (CD VI, 20–21). In this text, the love command functions as a central theme that is unpacked to show that such love is practical and includes support for the poor and needy as well as peaceful relations among the community. Much like in Jubilees (above), love toward others is how the righteous are to live. However, the second and more expansive love command—to love the stranger (Lev. 19:34)—is absent from the Damascus Document.

Another DSS that uses Leviticus 19:18 is Serekh (1QS), or Community Rule. While not directly quoting Leviticus, the text shows its influence by contrasting love and hate in a way that is very similar to Leviticus's teaching on how community members should love one another. Acknowledging that human beings will have conflict and disagreement, Serekh teaches members of the community not to speak in anger or out of jealousy or to hate one another, but rather to address wrongs by admonishing one another

> The Testaments of the Twelve Patriarchs were possibly written by Jews in the centuries before Jesus and added to by Christians, reaching their final form in the second century CE. They are similar to both Qumran texts and parts of the New Testament. There is much debate about which parts are Christianized, but there is no reason to think the allusion to the *shema* and Leviticus 19:18 are not part of the early Jewish form of the text.

with merciful love (1QS V, 24–VI, 1). Again the application of the command to love is very practical, although here applied primarily to relationships within the community.

Another set of Jewish texts come closer to what we find in the New Testament in combining the command to love God with

---

* Akiyama, *The Love of Neighbour in Ancient Judaism*, 96–132. For a longer list of other DSS texts that cite Leviticus 19:18, see Akiyama, 16.

love of neighbor.* The Testaments of the Twelve Patriarchs are twelve tracts in the names of the twelve tribes of Israel (Reuben, Simeon, Levi, Judah, and so on) exhorting the community to live ethically. One text instructs readers to keep the "law of God" and "love the Lord and your neighbor" (Testament of Issachar 5:1–2). Another commends speaking the truth to one's neighbor, peaceful living, and to "love the Lord through all your life and one another with a true heart" (Testament of Daniel 5:2–3). Other texts from this group allude more strongly to Leviticus 19, urging readers to "show mercy to your neighbor" so that God will be merciful to you (Testament of Zebulun 5:1). While none of these testaments explicitly or precisely quotes Deuteronomy 6:4 or Leviticus 19:18 in the way the gospel writers do, the sentiment is remarkably similar. Love of God and love of neighbor are a guiding ethic, paired inseparably for those who desire to follow God. Here we have a pre-Jesus tradition combining these two key Old Testament texts.

That the command to love God and neighbor was central to later Judaism can also be seen in the writings of Philo, a first-century CE Jewish philosopher. As a contemporary of Jesus and the authors of the New Testament, Philo can give us a sense of what other Jews were thinking at this time. In his treatise on the Jewish Law, Philo addresses the Ten Commandments, or "special laws," grouping them into two categories: (1) love of God and (2) love of neighbor (*On the Special Laws* 2.63). It seems that these two aspects of a life of faith had become a shorthand or summary for ethical obligation. Philo sounds very similar to the Jewish lawyer in Luke 10, who, when Jesus asks him what he reads in the Law, responds: "You shall love the Lord your God with all your heart, and with all your soul, and with all your strength, and with all your mind, and your neighbor as yourself."

* See DeSilva, "The Testaments of the Twelve Patriarchs as Witnesses to Pre-Christian Judaism: A Re-Assessment," *Journal for the Study of the Pseudepigrapha* 22, no. 4 (2013): 35–38, 51–55.

The Love Command in the New Testament ·

Having looked at the love command in Judaism up to the time of Jesus, we turn now to the New Testament. All three of the Synoptic Gospels (Matthew, Mark, and Luke) record a declaration about love of neighbor. Mark includes this teaching in a section of his gospel where Jesus is in conflict with other Jewish leaders. Jesus has argued with Sadducees about resurrection and now a scribe questions him about which commandment is the first. Jesus's response combines three of the most significant verses in the entire Old Testament to answer him:

- The LORD our God, the LORD is one (the *shema*, Deut. 6:4)
- Love the LORD your God with all your heart, life, and strength (Deut. 6:5)
- Love your neighbor as yourself (Lev. 19:18)

"There is no greater commandment than these," says Jesus (Mark 12:31). The oneness of God, loving God, and loving neighbor are combined to form the greatest or most important commandment in the Synoptic Gospel tradition. Despite the fact that the scribe probably disagrees with Jesus about many of his other teachings, strikingly, he agrees with him about this. "You are right," the scribe says, paraphrasing and repeating what Jesus has just said about love of God and neighbor being the greatest commandments. Despite their many differences, these two Jewish men are in complete agreement that the heart of faith can be summed up in the command to love.

Luke radically expands the command to love one's neighbor. His gospel contains a similar scene to Mark 12, in which a Jewish lawyer comes to Jesus to ask how to inherit eternal life (Luke 10:25–37). Jesus refers him to the *torah*—an appropriate move when talking to a lawyer! In Luke's Gospel the double love command is spoken by the lawyer, and Jesus affirms it. The twist comes when the lawyer, in typical lawyerly form, wants clarity about who constitutes his neighbor. It is a reasonable question and one debated in Jewish circles in terms of where the limits to ethical obligation lie. Jesus's response is to tell the story we know as the good Samaritan. The story begins with a traveler being attacked and left robbed, naked, beaten, and in need of help. Several of the religious leaders who pass by ignore the man, but a traveling Samaritan stops to help and is incredibly generous, even paying for his lodging and medical care until he recovers. The Samaritan is the hero of the story, the exemplar of the command to love one's neighbor. We need to remember Jesus is talking with fellow Jews here, and yet he makes an outsider (a Samaritan) the ideal. One's neighbor is redefined here as "the one who showed mercy" (Luke 10:37), not the one who lives geographically close by or the one who shares your religion, ethnicity, nationality, socioeconomic status, or gender. The biblical command to love "calls for concrete action rather than emotion or a lengthy theological or legal deliberation."*

The author of Matthew also has a version of this same story and also places the question in the mouth of a lawyer rather than a scribe (Matt. 22:34), but again puts his own particular spin on it. Matthew records the command to love God and to love neighbor (22:38–39), quoting Deuteronomy and Leviticus together, but in Matthew there seems to be an order: love of God comes first and is followed by love of neighbor. On these two, adds Matthew, "hang all the law and prophets" (22:40), in other words the entire Bible. Matthew has sharpened Mark's version of the story by adding this last comment, effectively making love of God and love of neighbor the hermeneutical (or interpretive) key to the entire Scripture. We will return to this below.

Paul, whose letters predate the gospels, likewise refers to the ethic to love God and neighbor in his letters. When writing to the Galatian churches about how to approach complex issues,

---

* Werner G. Jeanrond, *A Theology of Love* (London: T&T Clark, 2010), 34.

like the inclusion of those who are ethnically diverse and uncir-cumcised or the relationship between faith and law, he concludes his instructions by writing, "For the whole law is fulfilled in a sin-gle saying, 'You shall love your neighbor as yourself'" (Gal. 5:14). It is possible he knows that this is something Jesus taught or he is reflecting an agreed-upon ethic in first-century Judaism. He repeats the idea in his letter to the Romans, writing that the commandments are "summed up 'love your neighbor as yourself'" (Rom. 13:9). And just in case you missed the point the first time, Paul adds, "love is fulfilling the law [*torah*]" (Rom. 13:10).*

Paul's most famous passage on love is 1 Corinthians 13. It is often read at weddings although it is not primarily about romantic or family love but rather about how Christians are to live in the community. Having addressed the variety of spiri-tual gifts people receive, Paul urges this Christian community to "pursue love" (14:1) as the greatest gift (1 Cor. 13:13). Similar to the gospels, Paul presents love as based in action: patience, kind-ness, lack of irritability, lack of arrogance, and forbearance are all measurable behaviors, not feelings (1 Cor. 13:4–6). First Cor-inthians 13 is not the only place Paul talks about love as central to Christian life. In addition to these love behaviors addressed in 1 Corinthians 13, Paul writes elsewhere that love seeks peace-ful relationships (Gal. 6:1; Rom. 12:18), it does not harm others (Rom. 13:8–10), and it applies even to enemies (Rom. 12:20).

James likewise quotes Leviticus 19:18 when he preaches against favoritism in the Christian community, calling it the "royal law" (James 2:8). While that language might seem strange to us, we might translate this phrase as something like "the queen of laws" or "the supreme law." James appeals to Scripture as his authority, quoting the Greek version of Leviticus 19:18b: "If you fulfill the royal law according to the scripture 'love your neighbor as yourself,' you do well." Like Paul, James's letter pre-

---

* Love is also the first "fruit of the spirit" for those who belong to Jesus (Gal. 5:6, 22) precisely because it is the summation of the whole law.

sents love of neighbor as a summation of the law. And much like the teaching in Leviticus, the emphasis is on love toward those who are vulnerable in the community, such as orphans, widows, and the poor (James 1:27; 2:6).

John's Gospel does not quote Leviticus, but biblical scholars have long noted that love is a central theme in John.* Theologically, the author of John's Gospel portrays human love as grounded in God's love for the world (John 3:16–17), as something vital to the Father-Son relationship and therefore also to the relationship between believers (John 3:35–36; 5:20; 15:9; 17:23–26). Additionally, Jesus commands his followers to "love one another" at several points. All these commands to "love one another" in John occur as part of Jesus's farewell address, his final words to his disciples before his arrest, trial, and death (13:34–35; 15:12–17). As the departing words to his disciples, these passages indicate the principal elements of Jesus's teaching. The command to love is elucidated further by referring to Jesus's own love or action—it is to be done in imitation of Jesus. Followers are called to love like Jesus, a love exemplified in John's Gospel by Jesus's washing his disciples' feet (13:1–20) and by laying down his life (15:13). Finally, at the end of John's Gospel, Peter is commissioned to continue the work of Jesus, and it is framed as a commitment to love. "Do you love me?" Jesus asks Peter three times before telling him, "feed my sheep" (John 21:15–19). In John's Gospel, Jesus embodies the ethic that love of God and love of neighbor are inseparable. Such love is both practical and costly.

The centrality of love and the command to love one another takes on various forms in the later epistles of the New Testament. For example, in 1 John love is so closely connected with the divine that the author writes that "God is Love" (4:8, 16). In the book

---

* Christopher Skinner, "Love One Another: The Johannine Love Command in the Farewell Discourse," in *Johannine Ethics: The Moral World of the Gospel and Epistles of John* (Minneapolis: Fortress, 2017), 25–42.

of Revelation one community is admonished because they have "abandoned" their first love (Rev. 2:4), and another is commended for their love (2:19), while in the Letter to the Ephesians believers are instructed to "bear one another in love" (4:2). Much more could be said about the way the love command continues to function in the New Testament and into early Christian literature, but it is not the purpose of this book to offer a thoroughgoing investigation of the theme of love in the Bible (others have done so).* Rather, I hope to have shown how ubiquitous the command to love is and how Jesus and his first followers consistently emphasized this small verse of Scripture from Leviticus 19:18 in striking ways. The question now is, What does that matter? And does it have anything to do with the way we interpret the Bible?

LOVE AS HERMENEUTICAL KEY

Love is consistently portrayed as the key to Christian life in the New Testament, and we have seen that Leviticus 19:18b is not only quoted frequently but infuses the entire New Testament. Even more important for our purposes, however, is that the double love command (to love God and neighbor) becomes a guiding principle for interpretation in the New Testament. We see this most clearly in Matthew's Gospel, which refers to the love command three times (5:43; 19:19; 22:39), following each with additional commentary by Jesus. In Matthew 5, Jesus adds the command to include enemies in acts of love, praying for those who persecute or harm (5:43–45). In Matthew 19, Jesus again expands the idea of

---

* Victor Paul Furnish, *The Love Command in the New Testament* (London: SCM, 1973); Francis J. Moloney, *Love in the Gospel of John: An Exegetical, Theological, and Literary Study* (Grand Rapids: Baker Academic, 2013); Matthias Konradt, "The Love Command in Matthew, James, and the Didache," in *Matthew, James, and the Didache: Three Related Documents in Their Jewish and Christian Settings* (Atlanta: SBL Press, 2008), 271–88.

loving God and neighbor, telling the young man seeking eternal life that to really fulfill the law, "go sell your possessions and give the money to the poor" (19:21). To be perfect in loving one's neighbor is demanding, costly, and hard.* For a wealthy young man, it will involve giving what he has to those less fortunate. For someone else, the demand might be different. In this case, the wealthy young man walks away grieving. To love like God is difficult.

While all three Synoptic Gospels record Jesus teaching that the Torah can be summarized by the commands to love God and love your neighbor (Matt. 22; Mark 12; Luke 10), only Matthew adds that Jesus said, "On these two commands hang all the law and the prophets" (22:40). Remember that "law and prophets" is a way of referring to the whole Old Testament, the Bible of Jesus. The image here is of love as the hook upon which the words of the Bible hang and the key to unlocking the meaning of the Scriptures. If God's will is expressed through the prophets and authors of the Old Testament who wrote down the commandments, then Jesus is saying that love is the foundation, the glue, the heart of God's plan for humanity. Love is the guiding principle for interpreting the Bible.

Victor Furnish, author of *The Love Command in the New Testament*, defines love in Matthew's Gospel "as the key to the Law's meaning."† Another way to put this is if your interpretation of the law does not lead to acts of love, then it cannot be correct. Love is the check point and the goal of biblical interpretation.

I am by no means the first Christian to notice that love becomes a hermeneutical key to interpreting Scripture in the New Testament teachings of Jesus. In the fifth century, an African Christian bishop called Augustine dedicated large sections of his writings to unpacking what it means to love God, self, and neighbor.‡ Much

* Konradt, "The Love Command in Matthew, James, and the Didache," 276.
† Furnish, *The Love Command in the New Testament*, 195.
‡ For example, *Teaching Christianity* 1.20–44.

like the author of Matthew's Gospel, Augustine considers love the goal of any interpretation of the Bible. Augustine writes:

> What all that has been said amounts to, while we have been dealing with things, is that the fulfillment and the end of the law and of all divine scriptures is love. . . .
>
> So if it seems to you that you have understood the divine scriptures, or any part of them, in such a way that by this understanding you do not build up this twin love of God and neighbor, then you have not yet understood them. (*Teaching Christianity* 1.39–40)*

For Augustine, the point of interpreting and seeking to understand the Bible is to increase one's love of God and neighbor. If an interpretation does not lead to more love, then Augustine suggests one needs to go back and interpret again.†

Interestingly, Augustine acknowledges that one could interpret Scripture in a way that leads to more love but is not what the Bible really means. He says that such mistakes are "not pernicious" (or harmful).‡ Indeed, these mistakes, if they still lead to love, still lead to the goal of the law and get Christians to the same place, even if it's by another road. In other words, if we are

---

* John E. Rotelle, ed., *Teaching Christianity: De Doctrina Christiana*, trans. Edmund Hill (New York: New City Press, 1996). The Latin name *De doctrina christiana* has often been translated as *On Christian Doctrine*. It is not, however, a book about doctrine but a book about how to teach Christianity and the use of Scripture.

† Augustine assumes interpreters will also use other tools available, such as insights from reason and rhetoric, checking received translations, and reading the original Hebrew or Greek. To these more academic insights he adds wisdom, humility, and reliance on God. He also allows for multiple layers of meaning—Scripture can have both a literal and a figurative (spiritual) sense. See Rotelle, ed., *Teaching Christianity: De Doctrina Christiana*, 89.

‡ *Teaching Christianity* 1.40–41.

to err in our interpretation of Scripture—which, let's be honest, we all will at some point—it is better to err on the side of love. Centuries later, the Reformers, influenced by Augustine, would also emphasize love for God and one another as the goal of interpreting Scripture. By goal, I mean that reading and immersing oneself in the Bible should motivate one to love more. One might come to the Bible with personal concerns or an intellectual curiosity to understand a certain passage, but ultimately the Bible exists to draw its readers into relationship with God as well as to teach them how to live best with one another.

Martin Luther (1483–1546) famously argued that we use Scripture to interpret Scripture and that faith alone saves us. Because of this, God does not need our good works, he writes, but our neighbors do.* Living out the calling we hear in Scripture, for Luther, is living out love of God and neighbor. John Calvin (1509–1564) likewise emphasized the importance of Scripture for the Christian life and the need for individuals to be able to interpret it for themselves. Like the writers of the New Testament and Augustine before him, Calvin saw love as key to living out Christian vocation. Citing several of the biblical passages mentioned above, Calvin writes that love of neighbor is the "proof" we love God.†

Over in England, John Wesley (1703–1791) would also emphasize the importance of love in Christian life, albeit in a slightly different way. Wesley is famous for his emphasis on holiness (sanctification), which he closely associated with a now familiar biblical pair of commands—love God and love your neighbor. In his sermon *On Perfection*, Wesley quotes Matthew's Gospel, stating that on love of God and neighbor "hang all the law and prophets," and adds that "these contain the whole of Christian perfection."‡

* See Gustaf Wingren, *Luther on Vocation*, trans. Carl C. Rasmussen (Eugene, OR: Wipf and Stock, 2004).
† Calvin, *Institutes*, 2.8.53–54. See also his sermon on Galatians 5.
‡ Wesley, Sermon 76. *The Works of John Wesley*, vol. 3, ed. Albert C. Outler (Nashville: Abingdon, 1986), 74.

In his sermon titled *The Love of God*, Wesley preached that "love is the end of every commandment of Christ."* It is strikingly similar to Augustine's understanding that love is the goal of the Bible. Christian love is first and foremost oriented toward God for John Wesley but cannot be divorced from love toward humans. Loving God's creatures is part of loving God.† This love was not emotional nor abstract for Wesley, but concrete, ethical, and relational.‡ Good works do not earn salvation, but they are evidence of a Christian's love for God.

For these reformers, one cannot be a Christian without love of both God and neighbor. And while they articulate it in slightly different ways, there is a common thread that runs from the New Testament into the Reformation period via Augustine that argues that the goal of Scripture, and indeed a life of faith, is to produce more love for God and God's creation. Love is the key.

Conclusion

The disagreement I recounted at the beginning of this chapter was about biblical interpretation when it came to sexuality. My Christian brother came from a tradition that interprets the Bible in a literalistic way: the words on the page are believed to be normative and prescriptive for all time and should be applied literally wherever possible. For him that meant that anything other than heterosexual love within marriage was going to bring judgment and he wanted to save people from what he believed would be eternal damnation.

* Wesley, Sermon 144. *The Works of John Wesley*, vol. 4, ed. Albert C. Outler (Nashville: Abingdon, 1987), 332.

† Wesley, Sermon 144, p. 333; and Wesley, "A Plain Account of Christian Perfection," *The Works of John Wesley*, vol. 13, ed. Paul Wesley Chilcote and Kenneth J. Collins, 143.

‡ Mildred Bangs Wynkoop, *A Theology of Love: The Dynamic of Wesleyanism*, 2nd ed. (Kansas City: Beacon Hill Press, 2015).

I, however, interpret the Bible in the way I've been writing about: as a text with a living, dynamic history of being constantly (re)interpreted in conversation with the communities reading it. I read with one eye toward the historical context, understanding how it reflects ancient attitudes toward women, bodies, and sexuality, and one eye toward our own cultural values and the insights gained from science and medicine. Where there is difference, and there often is, these differences have to be carefully and prayerfully navigated to interpret faithfully. What guides that navigation is a core theological assumption that God embodies loving-kindness (the *khesed* I wrote about above) and wants us to do the same. I don't think that laws written for a different culture over 2,500 years ago should be considered normative for all time. I think the Bible itself gives us a mandate to keep interpreting for new times and places and that what constitutes the most loving and faithful action today is affirming LGBTIQ+ people. If I'm erring in that interpretation (and some of you will think I am), I am erring on the side of love.

In this chapter we have seen how one small part of Leviticus 19:18, "love your neighbor as yourself," became a central ethic in the New Testament. Jesus combined it with the command in Deuteronomy 6:5 to "love the LORD your God with all your heart" to proclaim a double love command that served as a summary of the entire Torah: love God and love neighbor. While Jesus was not the first Jew to formulate the love command as a way to summarize biblical teachings, this teaching was "central to Jesus's own message and mission."* As a result, the centrality of love in the New Testament as the characteristic of God that Christians are called to imitate cannot be overstated.

I have argued that in Matthew's Gospel, this ethic to love God and neighbor does not just govern general behavior but is the guiding principle for interpreting the Bible. The entirety of

* Furnish, *The Love Command*, 194.

Scripture "hangs" on love of God and neighbor. If we want to interpret the Bible like the Bible interprets itself, then our focus must be on interpretation that leads to loving God and loving our neighbor. As a hermeneutical ethic, it offers any interpreter of the Bible a guiding principle and goal. It is perhaps best posed as a question: Does this interpretation lead to more love of God and neighbor?

CHAPTER SEVEN

Reading the Bible for Love

For I desire loving kindness and not sacrifice,
the knowledge of God rather than burnt offerings.

— HOSEA 6:6

God is love, and those that abide in love abide in God
and God abides in them.

— 1 JOHN 4:16

It was a warm Monday in late summer, and I was spending it at an Islamic community center and mosque in Melbourne with some theological students. We were there as part of a course focused on learning about other faiths. After leading us through the main pillars of Islam, our host spoke about her own faith. She spoke with joy about her love for God and the role faith played in her own life. Then, acknowledging that submission to anything beyond ourselves is profoundly countercultural, she spoke about how a posture of submission to God was central for a Muslim. "If you remember one thing about Islam," she said, "remember the word 'submission.'" Then she asked us if there was one word that summarized Christianity. One student responded, "Love." She nodded and said, "That sounds right."

In the first few centuries, Christians were famous for their love. It is not that the surrounding cultures didn't love, but that Christian love was different because it crossed cultural and familial borders as new faith communities formed. In a letter written in the second century CE, an anonymous author writes about Christians: "They love everyone and are persecuted by all. They are not understood and they are condemned. They are put to death and made alive. They are impoverished and make many rich. They lack all things and yet abound in everything. They are dishonored and they are exalted in their dishonors. They are slandered and they are acquitted. They are reviled and they bless, mistreated and they bestow honor. They do good

What is the Bible

History of our faith

Teachings for living

Reassurance of God's
     grace & love

Basic
1 Instruction
Before
L Leaving
E this earth

Study Bible
Hebrew Bible - mostly what
Catholic Bible   Jesus would
                          have quoted
                   but most often
                   quoted from
                   Greek.

Words can become weapons

and are punished as evil."* This author, who simply calls himself a "disciple," writes to someone called Diognetus to show how Christians love. They love everyone, not just their kin, and their love extends even to enemies, against whom they do not retaliate and to whom they do good deeds. In a similar vein, another second-century Christian writer, called Tertullian, records that non-Christians are aghast when they look at the behavior of Christians. He quotes a Roman pagan exclaiming, "see how these Christians love one another."†

It is probably no longer the case that Christians are known for their love. Too often the view of Christianity from the outside, at least in the media and popular culture, is of a religion marked by judgment, homophobia, sexual abuse and subsequent cover-ups, anti-science views, misogyny, and even vaccine hesitancy. This is, of course, not the complete picture and does not do justice to the millions of Christians who perform daily acts of love and service in their communities. But, sadly, the point stands: we have moved a long way from being a group known primarily for our love. In between us and the earliest Christian communities stands a checkered history of colonialism, imperialism, crusades, conquest, patriarchy, and enslavement, all in the name of Jesus.

This history has influenced our biblical interpretation and so too has our institutional culture. Church leaders and preachers tend to want to protect the status quo and the power Christians in the West have garnered. Too often, Christians see cultural change as a threat to ecclesial and biblical authority and the Bible gets weaponized in response.

---

* *Letter to Diognetus* 5.11–16, in *The Apostolic Fathers*, vol. 2, trans. Bart D. Ehrman, LCL 25 (Cambridge, MA: Harvard University Press, 2003), 140–41.

† Tertullian, *Apology* 39.7. Whether Tertullian is actually quoting someone or using this rhetorically does not really matter. The point is that love is central to Christian faith.

How Did We Get Here?

When I was a young science major in the 1990s, one of the hot topics of Christian conversation was evolution. On the one hand, I had professors teaching me evolutionary theory and, on the other, campus ministry leaders telling me that "real Christians" rejected evolution in favor of Genesis 1's account of seven days of creation. This was all on the same university campus. In that particular campus ministry's approach to the Bible, Genesis 1 was read as a literal seven days of creation with no appreciation for the type of genre to which Genesis belongs or its theological purpose.* Genesis was upheld as a rival scientific account of creation, one that opposes Darwinism and evolutionary theory. I probably drove my professors crazy with my earnest attempts to combat evolution in class. I thought I had to choose between what I read in the Bible and what I was learning in my classes and that only one could be true. It took some years to realize that the Christian approach I had been taught set up an entirely unnecessary conflict between the Bible and science and that there was another way to read the Bible, one that allowed me to affirm a creator God and accept the insights of modern science with regards to evolutionary processes. One that took the Bible more seriously, not less.

How did we get into such conflicts between the Bible and science? In the seventeenth and eighteenth centuries, Enlightenment philosophers and scientists began to challenge accepted truths with their emphasis on reason and the scientific method rather than revelation. This inevitably affected the church and its interpretation of the Bible. At the risk of oversimplifying a complex story, reactions can be broadly grouped into two camps: those who rejected the claims of the Enlightenment and held up the Bible as the ultimate, infallible authority over all knowledge (conservatives) and those who adopted the methods of

* See my discussion of creation stories on pp. 68–75.

the Enlightenment and started interpreting the Bible with new "scientific" methods (liberals). The former reacted to Enlightenment thinking by positioning themselves against such changes. The latter group adopted its methods for a sacred text. Neither is a particularly good solution.

On the liberal side, biblical scholarship moved outside the control of the churches into university settings and developed more scientific methods for interpreting the Bible. While contributing wonderful insights and new tools, it also led to a nineteenth-century emphasis on the historical-critical method and the idea that if one just applied the right scientific methods, biblical scholarship could be objective, free from bias and personal beliefs. An inevitable impact of methods that prized the rational above all else was the questioning of the historicity of anything supernatural, like miracles or even the resurrection.

The famous "Jefferson Bible" is an excellent example of this nineteenth-century approach to the Bible. Later in his life, the US President Thomas Jefferson razor cut passages out of six copies of the New Testament and rearranged them to remove references to anything supernatural or miraculous.* Published as the *Life and Morals of Jesus of Nazareth*, Jefferson's revised Bible consisted of passages from the four gospels that highlight the teachings of Jesus, omit the miracles, and minimize the supernatural.† The ongoing impact of this kind of liberalism can be found in preaching that explains away miracles—the feeding of the five thousand becomes a miracle of everyone sharing their secret stash of food, and Jesus walking on water becomes him walking on a sandbar to create an illusion—or in disdain for belief in the virgin birth and even the resurrection of Jesus.

---

* https://www.smithsonianmag.com/smithsonian-institution/why-thomas-jefferson-created-his-own-bible-180975716/.

† For example, the birth of Jesus is told without reference to angelic involvement.

Liberal approaches have dominated and continue to dominate biblical scholarship, leading to sometimes-dismissive attitudes toward theological questions as well as the supernatural aspects of the text. Most biblical scholars now grant that objectivity is unattainable and recognize that Jesus's teaching cannot be divorced from his miraculous deeds if we want to understand what the gospel writers are conveying. Good historical scholarship accounts for the way belief in the supernatural is assumed and reflected in the Bible in ways that may not make sense for modern science but do not have to. The legacy of liberalism on the church, however, persists.

At the other end of the spectrum lies the conservative approach. Ironically, even those who rejected the claims of the Enlightenment could not help but be influenced by it and, indeed, adopt its assumptions. The idea of "truth" became identified with the kinds of facts that could be established by the scientific method (as opposed to a broader notion of truth that might allow for spiritual wisdom or mystical experience). If the Bible was "true," thought the conservatives, then this meant it had to be factually true, that is, historically and scientifically unassailable. What followed was the rise of fundamentalism, doctrines of inerrancy, and approaches to the Bible that used science and archaeology to try and prove its narrative. For example, there have been searches for the archaeological remains of Noah's Ark. These approaches still dominate large parts of Protestant evangelical Christianity.* Instead of appealing to the spiritual or theological truths of the Bible, conservative Protestants have tried to play the game on Enlightenment terms and have been engaged in culture wars ever since.

* A contemporary example of this is the Museum of the Bible in Washington, DC, which showcases artifacts spanning four thousand years of history to help give visitors "an immersive and personalized experience with the Bible" and whose pre-2012 website mission statement said their aim was "to inspire confidence in the absolute authority and reliability of the Bible."

In addition to the aforementioned science-evolution-creationism debate that has plagued some Christian circles for decades now, a comparable culture war was and is being waged over gender roles. As wider society began to change its views and give women more equal rights under the influence of feminism, conservative Christian authorities responded by protecting their (male) power and trying to stamp out a similar rise of feminism within the church. They did so by introducing the notion of "complementarianism" in the late 1980s—the idea that each gender has a distinct but complementary role, where men lead or have "headship" in both domestic and public spaces, and women fulfill support roles.* Under this theological worldview, women like myself, who have a sense of call to ministry, are told that leadership is intended by God for men. The selective and literalistic use of the Bible as a form of proof for those arguing this view demonstrates how much complementarians have adopted the terms of the Enlightenment. In this approach, the Bible becomes a proof text, a book of facts that can be mined for evidence without regard for the cultural, historical, or literary complexities of any given passage.

The hardening of positions on science and gender as well as the insistence on an entirely literal interpretation of the Bible are both relatively new historical phenomena and a direct reaction to the scientific revolution. They turn the Bible into something it never was. Many modern Christians have convinced themselves that belief is most correct and the Bible is most powerful when understood and defended as a set of facts. To treat the

---

* Piper and Grudem's *Recovering Biblical Manhood and Womanhood: A Response to Evangelical Feminism* does not hide the fact that it is reacting to feminism. It's right there in the title! See John Piper and Wayne Grudem, eds., *Recovering Biblical Manhood and Womanhood: A Response to Evangelical Feminism* (Wheaton: Crossway, 1991) and a history of complementarianism in Beth Allison Barr's *The Making of Biblical Womanhood: How the Subjugation of Women Became Gospel Truth* (Grand Rapids: Brazos, 2021).

Bible as a series of facts, however, is to reduce its possibilities and to diminish its power. It also reduces truth to that which is scientifically verifiable and ignores the complex contexts from which it emerged and into which it speaks. That is, treating the Bible as facts ignores its very nature.

This brief history explains why some parts of the Christian church have actually become more conservative in the last few decades while others have embraced women's leadership and the insights of science in relation to creation, gender, sexuality, and climate change. Today the pendulum is swinging as notable evangelical leaders are pushing back on fundamentalist readings of the Bible and evangelical women are critiquing male headship as unbiblical and dangerous because of its propensity for abuse. Conversely, those on the more liberal side are recognizing the limits of the scientific method when applied to a deeply theological text. Newer voices are asking questions about gender, power, culture, race, and politics in ways that deepen and challenge existing interpretations and notions of objectivity. When we consider the history of interpretation embedded in the Bible itself, we see that these (new) approaches are deeply faithful to the biblical tradition. Instead of seeing cultural change as a threat to ecclesial and biblical authority, such approaches see contemporary questions as an opportunity to continue the task of interpreting the Bible for new audiences and new contexts.

INTERPRETING FOR LOVE IN TODAY'S WORLD

In the midst of all this change and the plethora of tools at our disposal to interpret the Bible, I began this project looking for a guiding principle, a biblical ethic that might guide our collective interpretation. What I discovered in the Bible is a prevailing ethic of love for God and neighbor. So, I leave you with two key questions that can be asked of any biblical passage and should be asked of any interpretation of the Bible:

1. How does this interpretation lead me to love God more?
2. How does this interpretation lead me to love my neighbor more?

These questions do not negate the need for being attentive to translation and linguistic complexities, the historical and cultural setting, or the literary style of any biblical text. Neither do they negate the need to be prayerful, humble, and communal when we interpret the Bible, as I discussed in chapter 2. Ideally, we bring all our best tools with us as we seek to understand the Word of God. Neither are these questions the only questions we can or should ask of the biblical text. But I would argue they are a good check point and that the Bible itself, as well as the early Christian tradition, prioritizes love and considers it the goal of reading the Bible. What if that was our goal too? What might a hermeneutic of love look like?

To interpret the Bible through the lens of love first means we read with compassion, aligning ourselves with those in the text with whom we might not naturally connect. We try and read with a spirit of generosity toward the views of others both in the text and in the tradition to see what it might provoke in us. The more we do this, the more we learn about what it means to love God and neighbor from the Bible itself.

Second, we do no harm. We do not use the Bible to justify the oppression of others. In efforts to control people, set boundaries, or compel faith, the Christian church has historically engaged in awful behaviors that have abused, oppressed, and hurt people. In the Americas, white Christians used the Bible to justify slavery and, later, segregation. One common interpretation was that the "mark of Cain" (Gen. 4:15) was dark skin.* When put alongside the curse of Ham (Gen. 9:20–25), a passage that condemns Ham's offspring to slavery, Christian leaders argued that Black people were destined by God

* The mark of Cain is about divine protection from being killed.

for slavery.* In South Africa, the Dutch Reformed Church similarly used the Bible to justify apartheid, arguing the Bible endorses the separation of races. Acts 17:26, which speaks of God allotting "the boundaries of the places where they [the nations] would live" was frequently cited.† The same verse, among others, was being invoked in Australia, where the Bible was used on both sides of the 1940s debate about the Immigration Restriction Act, a policy that sought to exclude non-Europeans from migration to Australia in an endeavor to maintain a "white Australia."‡ If we are honest about our history, Christians need to not only repent of past abuses and seek reconciliation where possible but also learn from it and reflect on the ways we might be continuing to hurt people due to our own biases or desires to protect power and privilege. We need to stop using the Bible to harm and oppress others.

Third, a hermeneutic of love means we ask how any particular biblical passage might lead us to loving action toward our neighbors today. This can take some careful work. While some parts of the Bible contain clear moral or ethical teaching, others invite us into a more reflective exercise. How does the way we react to a passage, character, or story reveal our own biases and the areas where we lack compassion? How is the text a mirror

---

* In nineteenth-century Australia, Christians similarly argued that the Indigenous peoples descended from Noah and bore the curse of Ham. See Meredith Lake, *The Bible in Australia: A Cultural History* (Sydney: NewSouth, 2018), 100.

† Inversely, Acts 17:26 was used by Christian humanitarians to contest racism and argue for racial equality. In this case the emphasis was usually placed on the earlier part of the verse "from one ancestor God made all nations." See Lake, *The Bible in Australia*, 96.

‡ Lake, *The Bible in Australia*, 237–39. It is worth noting that Australia was never "white." Aboriginal and Torres Strait Islander peoples lived in what we now call Australia for thousands of years prior to the arrival of white people.

for our own experiences? Where does it expose our lack of love? Where does it compel us to grow?

Fourth, we prioritize compassion toward people over rituals, rules, institutions, and commands, even biblical ones. That last one might seem shocking, but Paul did precisely that when he argued that the biblical commands to circumcise all men and to keep certain food laws no longer applied as God was doing a new thing in calling gentile believers to faith in Jesus Christ (see Gal. 2–3). It was profoundly controversial at the time, and some of his fellow Jews thought he had completely "sold out" to culture. Paul, however, argued in favor of radical inclusion on the basis of his own experience of God's grace and mercy. The contemporary church does likewise when it permits divorce and presides over the marriages of divorcees. Jesus said little about marriage or sexual relationships, but one of the few recorded comments is a teaching denouncing the divorce practices of his time (Mark 10:2–12). One could read this as a prohibition of divorce, but many contemporary Christian churches have interpreted it as contextual and allow divorce in an acknowledgment that relationships are complex, we humans make mistakes and hurt one another, and attitudes to marriage and divorce have changed. That is, churches that permit divorce have chosen the side of mercy and inclusion in a hermeneutical move that mimics Paul's teaching on circumcision.

There is arguably no more controversial or fraught issue of interpretation for the contemporary church than that relating to sexuality and how to interpret passages in the Bible that condemn homosexual activities. Too often interpreters have applied such texts literally and in doing so have failed to listen with compassion to LGBTIQ+ people and their experiences, have used the Bible to justify harm, and have ignored insights from modern medicine that suggest profoundly different understandings of sexuality to those of 2,500 years ago. If we try to interpret the Bible in the way the Bible interprets itself, with a focus on loving God and loving neighbor, our interpretation would look different. We might recognize the need to reinterpret for new contexts and that a loving interpretation, at minimum, does not cause harm to others. While most Christians balk at forcing shock therapy on young gay and lesbian people, many continue to harm through teaching and spiritual practices that cause people to hate themselves and question whether they can be loved by God or indeed by other people.* This kind of theology is not love. It can be abusive and cause long-term damage. On the contrary, love means beginning with a stance of compassion and mercy that prioritizes people and their own experiences. It begins with listening in love and embracing the other, not because we are all the same but precisely because we are different from one another. Interpreting through the lens of love asks two simple questions—Does this interpretation increase love of God? Does this interpretation increase my love of other humans?

Fifth, we might ask how a passage and its interpretation leads us to more love for God. What does it reveal about the nature of God and how does it challenge our ideas about God? How might we respond—perhaps with prayer or worship? How does it shape our relationship with the divine?

Let's look at an example of what such an approach might look like.

Interpreting the David and Bathsheba Story (2 Samuel 11)

¹In the spring of the year, the time when kings go out to battle, David sent Joab with his officers and all Israel with him; they

---

* Survivors of practices that intend to change their sexuality say that things like prayer and the laying on of hands are often experienced as abusive or traumatic and cause them to doubt themselves when they are not able to change. See for example the reports of survivors in the SOGICE Survivor Statement, www.socesurvivors.com.au.

ravaged the Ammonites, and besieged Rabbah. But David remained at Jerusalem. ²It happened, late one afternoon, when David rose from his couch and was walking about on the roof of the king's house, that he saw from the roof a woman bathing; the woman was very beautiful. ³David sent someone to inquire about the woman. It was reported, "This is Bathsheba daughter of Eliam, the wife of Uriah the Hittite." ⁴So David sent messengers to get her, and she came to him, and he lay with her. (Now she was purifying herself after her period.) Then she returned to her house. ⁵The woman conceived; and she sent and told David, "I am pregnant." (NRSV)

This famous story begins with the narrator telling us that the country is at war but King David has remained in Jerusalem. This is unusual for a king, who would normally ride out into battle with his troops. Instead, David is walking on his rooftop when he sees Bathsheba for the first time. Bathsheba is bathing in her own space, presumably her home, and is washing or purifying herself.*

In the stark telling in the Bible, David is the active character and all the verbs describe what he does: he "sees" her bathing and "sends" someone to inquire about her. The narrator's voice tells us she is exceedingly beautiful. When told she is Eliam's daughter and Uriah's wife, David sends messengers and "takes," "enters," and "sleeps with" her (2 Sam. 11:4 LXX, my trans.). The fact that she is already married to one of his military leaders is not

---

* There is scholarly debate about what the text means when it refers to her washing and "purifying" or "sanctifying herself" (11:4). Some think she is ritually washing after her period, although there is no historical evidence this was the practice at the time. Other scholars think she is just taking a regular bath, and others, like Chankin-Gould et al., have argued she was sanctifying herself in the manner of a deity. See J. D. Chankin-Gould et al., "The Sanctified 'Adulteress' and Her Circumstantial Clause: Bathsheba's Bath and Self-Consecration in 2 Samuel 11," *Journal for the Study of the Old Testament* 32, no. 3 (March 1, 2008): 339–52.

a deterrent for David. She goes home but later sends word she is pregnant. In the story that follows, David recalls Uriah from the battlefield and tries to get him to sleep with his wife to hide the source of the pregnancy. When Uriah refuses on the grounds that he should not get to enjoy such things while his men are away on the battlefield, David arranges to have him killed.

Christian interpreters of this passage have tended to interpret this story in one of three ways: Bathsheba is a seductress who uses her beauty to get close to the king in order to gain power; David and Bathsheba commit adultery together;* or David rapes Bathsheba, then murders her husband to cover it up. The first blames Bathsheba, drawing on the trope of women as sexual temptresses and men as hapless victims of female sexual power; the second holds them mutually accountable and implies they both sin; and the third places the blame firmly at David's feet, recognizing Bathsheba as a victim of rape. Where might a hermeneutic of love lead us?

1. *Reading with compassion for the characters.* An interpretation that seeks to love Bathsheba is one that seeks to understand her circumstances and imaginatively wonder what it might have been like for her. We might wonder whether she felt particularly vulnerable with her husband away. Was she terrified, delighted, or confused when summoned to the palace? Could she have refused the king? Could she have cried for help if she'd wanted to once David's desires became clear? The text doesn't tell us much from her point of view, except that she reports her pregnancy. What does she expect from David in doing so? We don't really

---

* For example, the NRSV Bible labels this story, "David commits adultery with Bathsheba," and many of the major commentaries use similar headings. Rarely is the word *rape* used in commentaries other than feminist or womanist ones. For example, womanist scholar Wil Gafney summarizes this story as "the abduction, rape, and forced impregnation of Bathsheba." (Womanist means feminist of color.) https://www.wil gafney.com/2019/03/05/ritualizing-bathshebas-rape/.

know. Historically, a woman in her position could probably not refuse a king. The power differential between her and David was enormous. Moreover, she lived in a patriarchal world where women were expected to be obedient to men, be they fathers or husbands or other male leaders. Bathsheba was put in a terrible situation. She could not consent (in modern terms), nor could she say no. Her body belonged to her husband and now to the king. To read Bathsheba with compassion is to have sympathy for her and anyone in her situation.

To read with compassion for characters means we need to extend the same to David. We do not get to "cancel" him. We cannot write him off as an evil human being for whom these actions are all defining, but neither do we let him off the hook. We might recognize that when one is given enormous power, it is very easy to abuse that power. We might wonder if this is something David did regularly. Did David even recognize such actions as harmful to others or did he think he was behaving like a king should? We might also wonder why learning Bathsheba was Uriah's wife did not give him pause.

When we read each of these main characters in a way that tries to put us in their position, we start to humanize them and see them as whole human beings. We might even recognize ourselves in them and wonder, When have we abused our power?

2. *Doing no harm.* In some of the traditional interpretations mentioned above, this story gets used to perpetuate theologies that harm. If the story is interpreted to say that Bathsheba deliberately put herself on display to seduce David (something for which there is no evidence in the text), then the implication is that women's sexuality is dangerous and must be controlled and contained. This has a long and problematic legacy of oppressive attitudes toward women and their bodies. It does not do service to men either. In that interpretation, men, like David, are powerless in the face of female beauty. The "I was weak" excuse has been used by more than one Christian leader as a

way of minimizing their adultery or abuse. At its worst, such interpretations enable the church to turn a blind eye to abuse. If King David behaved so badly yet was still remembered as a good king, then perhaps it is all right to overlook other men who occasionally abuse their power. After all, so the logic goes, no one is perfect.

Reading with a hermeneutic of love allows us to critique those readings that do not lead to more love and instead lead to potential harm. To blame Bathsheba or minimize David's abuse is to perpetuate problematic stereotypes that blame women for their own abuse. It potentially leads us to disbelieve or blame women when they say they've been sexually abused and to excuse and protect those in power.

3. *Reading in our contexts.* How does this passage help me love my neighbor? What loving action might emerge? Here we move from the text to our contemporary settings. When we read Bathsheba with compassion for her circumstance, we read with the experiences of abused women everywhere. To do so is to listen to their experiences and let them inform our understanding. This goes beyond fostering understanding and compassion. One thing this passage prompts, for me, is the need to be a better supporter and advocate for women (and men) who have been abused, to believe their stories, to remind them they are loved and loveable, and to not shirk from naming the horror of abuse—even from the pulpit.

To read the story of Bathsheba's rape with an eye toward loving one's neighbor also prompts us to work for a world where no woman is raped and where women are no longer seen as objects to be taken or as subject solely to the desires of men.

Part of love is acting with honesty, accountability, and integrity. After all, Jesus's manner of love was deeply compassionate and merciful, but also challenged and called people to be better when they sinned. William Sloane Coffin writes that the prophets show "how frequently compassion demands confrontation. Love without criticism is a kind of betrayal."* Interpretations that have sought to rescue David's reputation smack of the kind of cover-ups of sexual abuse that continue in today's church. They fail to love or to show compassion toward survivors of abuse and perpetuate a warped "love" of power. To interpret this story with love for today's church is to be prepared to name and unveil problematic uses and abuses of power, to hold leaders accountable, and to do so even when our identity might be bound up with theirs. Too often Christians, under a guise of "niceness" or a desire to protect the institutional church, are bystanders to abuse. A hermeneutic of love does not allow us to be bystanders to injustice.

Lastly, interpreting David's action with love challenges us to think about ways we might support abusers who seek to address their behavior and recognize they too need God's love and forgiveness to become whole human beings. After all, even David, the rapist and murderer, is included in God's gracious mercy.

4. *Prioritizing people over institutions, rituals, or laws.* Not every biblical passage will have something to say to each of these points, but here I reiterate the point above. To prioritize people over institutions is to expose abuses of power, whatever they might look like. Where we have a choice between the institution or the person, we choose the person. Where we can be more loving rather than going to maximum judgment or punishment, choose that likewise. Choose mercy. According to biblical law, Bathsheba and David could both have been stoned for adultery (Lev. 20:10–12; Deut. 22:22–24). Interestingly, that is not what happens. If it had, David and Bathsheba would not have had more children (including King Solomon), Israel would have lost a king, and two lives would have been ended.

5. *How does this text help us love God more?* Here we might ask some questions about how God is portrayed in the passage

---

* William Sloane Coffin, *Credo* (Louisville: Westminster John Knox, 2004), 22.

or what it suggests about the nature of God. We can then ask ourselves how we might respond to that insight.

In the case of 2 Samuel 11, God seems quiet. God's voice will come later through the prophet Nathan, who confronts David with his sin. So my question in this case is less about God's activity in the narrative (as important as that is) and more about how reading this story with love might increase one's love for God. This is obviously both personal and subjective, but here is my reflection: the fact that this story portraying King David in such a terrible light is in the Bible at all reminds me that God works with deeply flawed human beings. If there is hope of recovery for someone like David, there is hope for someone like me to also experience God's forgiveness and grace. It also evokes a kind of awe in me at the very nature of a God who would continue to love, call, and show mercy to humanity even when we are terrible to one another.

Alongside that, this passage reminds me that God is a God of justice. David might not get the punishment some of us think he deserved (there's that mercy stuff again), but he does get confronted about his behavior and it is not without consequences. Lastly, that this story remains in the Bible gives me hope that women's voices and the experiences of the marginalized and abused are not lost to God. They are remembered by God, as are we all. For that mercy, I can only respond with more love.

Conclusion

I was a nineteen-year-old undergraduate science major when I experienced God calling me to ministry. While I'd had spiritual experiences before, this one remains the most vivid. It was mid-semester break and I was at a Christian conference for college students where the keynote speaker spoke about the church's need for leaders, for people called to serve Jesus's church. As he was speaking, I felt what can only be described as a jolt to my sleepy, half-attentive brain and a voice telling me, "That's what you will do." I looked around the room. No one else had changed posture or flinched, but my world felt like it had just been flipped upside down. I can't explain it, but I knew that voice was God's.

For context, I had been praying to God for years, asking what to do with my life, trying to discern what my calling or purpose could be. I pursued science because I could, not because I had any great passion for it. I am also a preacher's kid, so while church ministry was familiar, it was definitely not the answer to prayer I was looking for! I was hoping for something I perceived to be a more glamorous calling, like a medical missionary serving remote communities overseas or running an orphanage in Kenya or Nepal. God had other plans.

The irony is that the keynote speaker that day did not believe in the ordination of women and, at the time, neither did I. God had the audacity to call a woman who did not believe in the ordination of women to ordained ministry through a man who also did not believe in the ordination of women. Obviously, this required a reevaluation of some of my firmly held beliefs. So began a journey revisiting the Bible I held so dear to discover I had missed passages that spoke about the ministry of women like Mary, Junia, Miriam, and Prisca. Likewise, I learned that there were other ways to interpret the passages that seemed to silence or limit women, ways that accounted for cultural norms in the first century CE or took account of the whole message rather than only one verse. I began to read and reread. And while the way I read the Bible has shifted, deepened, and become more complicated, I am no less compelled by its power and message.

I started this project wanting to see how the Bible talked about interpretation and how it modeled interpretation. Given how divided the modern church can be when it comes to interpreting parts of the Bible, I wanted to see if there was a guiding ethic or principle within the Scriptures themselves. I set out to read the Bible on its own terms. What I discovered is that the Bible itself includes and embodies interpretation. Vast amounts of our received Bible are already interpretation of other parts of our Bible. These interpretations are a way of keeping the tradition alive, they represent diverse voices and contexts, and they routinely update earlier interpretations of the Bible. The common thread is that interpretation of God's Word for each new context is part of the dynamic nature of the text and of human experience of the divine.

When we stop trying to make the Bible into something it is not, we encounter a text that is a diverse, vibrant, living, breathing, wondrous thing. It is a text that almost demands we reinterpret it so that it can continue to speak. To be faithful to that tradition is not to assume all correct interpretation stopped in the first century CE or at some other key point in history. It is to know that as readers and interpreters of the Bible, we stand in a dynamic tradition. Respecting the authority of the Bible is, paradoxically, interpreting and reinterpreting it in conversation with the modern world.

Amidst the diversity of ways the biblical authors interpreted other biblical authors, an ethic emerges: love of God and love of neighbor. This, the greatest of commandments, is also the hermeneutical key. If our interpretation does not lead to love, we have, frankly, missed the point.

Bibliography

Akiyama, Kengo. *The Love of Neighbour in Ancient Judaism: The Reception of Leviticus 19:18 in the Hebrew Bible, the Septuagint, the Book of Jubilees, the Dead Sea Scrolls, and the New Testament.* Ancient Judaism and Early Christianity 105. Boston: Brill, 2018.

Andrews, James A. *Hermeneutics and the Church: In Dialogue with Augustine.* Notre Dame: University of Notre Dame Press, 2012.

Armstrong, Karen. *On the Bible.* Books That Shook the World. Crows Nest, NSW: Allen & Unwin, 2007.

Barr, Beth Allison. *The Making of Biblical Womanhood: How the Subjugation of Women Became Gospel Truth.* Grand Rapids: Brazos, 2021.

Bird, Michael F. *Romans.* Story of God Bible Commentary 6. Grand Rapids: Zondervan, 2016.

Bobertz, Charles, and David Brakke, eds. *Reading in Christian Communities: Essays on Interpretation in the Early Church.* Christianity and Judaism in Antiquity 14. Notre Dame: University of Notre Dame Press, 2002.

Boda, Mark J., and Paul L. Redditt, eds. *Unity and Disunity in Ezra-Nehemiah.* Hebrew Bible Monographs 17. Sheffield: Sheffield Phoenix Press, 2008.

Brueggemann, Walter, and Tod Linafelt. *An Introduction to the Old Testament: The Canon and Christian Imagination.* Louisville: Westminster John Knox, 2012.

Cadwallader, Alan H. *Hermeneutics and the Authority of Scripture.* Adelaide: ATF Press, 2011.

Carey, Greg. *Using Our Outside Voices: Public Biblical Interpretation.* Minneapolis: Fortress, 2020.

Carson, D. A., and H. G. M. Williamson, eds. *It Is Written: Scripture Citing Scripture. Essays in Honour of Barnabas Lindars.* Cambridge: Cambridge University Press, 1988.

Chambers, Alan. *My Exodus from Fear to Grace.* Grand Rapids: Zondervan, 2015.

Chankin-Gould, J. D'Ror, Derek Hutchinson, David Hilton Jackson, Tyler D. Mayfield, Leah Rediger Schulte, Tammi J. Schneider, and E. Winkleman. "The Sanctified 'Adulteress' and Her Circumstantial Clause: Bathsheba's Bath and Self-Consecration in 2 Samuel 11." *Journal for the Study of the Old Testament* 32, no. 3 (2008): 339–52.

Chilcote, Paul Wesley, and Kenneth J. Collins, eds. *The Works of John Wesley.* Vol. 13. Nashville: Abingdon, 2013.

Coffin, William Sloane. *Credo.* Louisville: Westminster John Knox, 2004.

Collins, John J. *What Are Biblical Values? What the Bible Says on Key Ethical Issues.* New Haven, CT: Yale University Press, 2019.

Davis, Ellen F. "Critical Traditioning: Seeking an Inner Biblical Hermeneutic." *Anglican Theological Review* 82, no. 4 (2000): 733–51.

DeSilva, David Arthur. "The Testaments of the Twelve Patriarchs as Witnesses to Pre-Christian Judaism: A Re-Assessment." *Journal for the Study of the Pseudepigrapha* 22, no. 4 (2013): 21–68.

Dunn, James D. G. *Romans.* Vol. 2. Dallas: Word Books, 1988.

Edgar, David Hutchinson. "The Use of the Love-Command and the Shema in the Epistle of James." *Proceedings of the Irish Biblical Association* 23 (2000): 9–22.

Enns, Peter E. *The Bible Tells Me So: Why Defending Scripture Has Made Us Unable to Read It.* New York: HarperOne, 2015.

———. *How the Bible Actually Works.* New York: HarperOne, 1989.

———. *Inspiration and Incarnation: Evangelicals and the Problem of the Old Testament.* Grand Rapids: Baker, 2005.

Bibliography

Epp, Eldon Jay. *Junia: The First Woman Apostle*. Minneapolis: Fortress, 2005.

Fishbane, Michael. *Biblical Interpretation in Ancient Israel*. Oxford: Oxford University Press, 1985.

Frey, Jörg. *The Letter of Jude and Second Letter of Peter: A Theological Commentary*. Waco, TX: Baylor University Press, 2018.

Furnish, Victor Paul. *The Love Command in the New Testament*. London: SCM, 1973.

Gabbay, Uri. "Hebrew Śôm Śekel (Neh. 8:8) in Light of Aramaic and Akkadian." *Journal of Semitic Studies* 59, no. 1 (2014): 47–51.

Grant, Robert M. *A Short History of the Interpretation of the Bible*. London: A & C Black, 1965.

Harper, Robert, ed. *The Code of Hammurabi, King of Babylon, about 2250 B.C.* Chicago: University of Chicago Press, 1904.

Hays, Richard B. *Echoes of Scripture in the Gospels*. Waco, TX: Baylor University Press, 2016.

Held Evans, Rachel. *Inspired: Slaying Giants, Walking on Water, and Loving the Bible Again*. Nashville: Nelson, 2018.

Høgenhaven, Jesper, Jesper Tang Nielsen, and Heike Omerzu, eds. *Rewriting and Reception in and of the Bible*. Wissenschaftliche Untersuchungen zum Neuen Testament 396. Tübingen: Mohr Siebeck, 2018.

Hoppe, Leslie J. "Biblical Interpretation in Ancient Israel: An Introduction." *Biblical Research* 35 (1990): 37–43.

House, H. Wayne. "Biblical Inspiration in 2 Timothy 3:16." *Bibliotheca Sacra* 137, no. 545 (1980): 54–63.

Hultin, Jeremy F. "The Literary Relationship among 1 Peter, 2 Peter, and Jude." In *Reading 1–2 Peter and Jude: A Resource for Students*, 27–45. Resources for Biblical Study 77. Atlanta: Society of Biblical Literature, 2014.

Jeanrond, Werner G. *A Theology of Love*. London: T&T Clark, 2010.

Keener, Craig S. "Greek versus Jewish Conceptions of Inspiration and 2 Timothy 3:16." *Journal of the Evangelical Theological Society* 63, no. 2 (June 2020): 217–31.

———. *The Gospel of Matthew: A Socio-Rhetorical Commentary*. Grand Rapids: Eerdmans, 2009.

Keith, Chris. *Jesus Against the Scribal Elite: The Origins of Conflict.* London: T&T Clark, 2020.

Knoppers, Gary N. "Treasures Won and Lost: Royal (Mis)appropriations in Kings and Chronicles." In *The Chronicler as Author: Studies in Text and Textures*, edited by M. Patrick Graham and Steven L. McKenzie, 181–208. Sheffield, UK: Sheffield Academic Press, 1999.

Konradt, Matthias. "The Love Command in Matthew, James, and the Didache." In *Matthew, James, and the Didache: Three Related Documents in Their Jewish and Christian Settings*, 271–88. Atlanta: SBL Press, 2008.

Kugel, James. *How to Read the Bible: A Guide to Scripture, Then and Now*. New York: Free Press, 2007.

Kugel, James L., and Rowan A. Greer. *Early Biblical Interpretation*. Philadelphia: Westminster, 1986.

Lake, Meredith. *The Bible in Australia: A Cultural History*. Sydney: New South Publishing, 2018.

Law, David R. *Inspiration of the Scriptures*. London: Continuum, 2001.

Levine, Amy-Jill, and Marc Zvi Brettler. *The Bible with and without Jesus: How Jews and Christians Read the Same Stories Differently*. New York: HarperCollins, 2020.

Levinson, Bernard M. *Deuteronomy and the Hermeneutics of Legal Innovation*. Oxford: Oxford University Press, 1998.

Loader, William R. G. *Jesus and the Fundamentalism of His Day*. Grand Rapids: Eerdmans, 2001.

———. *Jesus Left Loose Ends: Collected Essays*. Adelaide: ATF Press, 2021.

———. *Jesus's Attitude towards the Law: A Study of the Gospels*. Wissenschaftliche Untersuchungen zum Neuen Testament 2. Tübingen: Mohr Siebeck, 1997.

Ludlow, Morwenna. "'Criteria of Canonicity' and the Early Church." In *Die Einheit der Schrift und die Vielfalt Des Kanons—The*

Plurality of the Canon and Unity of the Bible, 69–93. Berlin: Walter de Gruyter, 2003.

Marcus, Joel. *Mark 1–8*. Anchor Yale Bible. New York: Doubleday, 2002.

Martin, Dale B. "Arsenokoites and Malakos: Meanings and Consequences." In *Biblical Ethics and Homosexuality*, 117–36. Louisville: Westminster John Knox, 1996.

———. *Biblical Truths: The Meaning of Scripture in the Twenty-First Century*. New Haven, CT: Yale University Press, 2017.

Mellinkoff, Ruth. *The Horned Moses in Medieval Art and Thought*. Berkeley: University of California Press, 1970.

Mitchell, Margaret Mary. *Paul and the Emergence of Christian Textuality: Early Christian Literary Culture in Context*. Wissenschaftliche Untersuchungen zum Neuen Testament 393. Tübingen: Mohr Siebeck, 2017.

Moloney, Francis J. *Love in the Gospel of John: An Exegetical, Theological, and Literary Study*. Grand Rapids: Baker Academic, 2013.

Mroczek, Eva. "Hezekiah the Censor and Ancient Theories of Canon Formation." *Journal of Biblical Literature* 140, no. 3 (2021): 481–502.

———. *The Literary Imagination in Jewish Antiquity*. Oxford: Oxford University Press, 2016.

Mtata, Kenneth, and Craig R. Koester, eds. *To All the Nations: Lutheran Hermeneutics and the Gospel of Matthew*. Lutheran World Federation Studies. Leipzig: Lutheran World Federation, 2015.

Najman, Hindy. *Seconding Sinai: The Development of Mosaic Discourse in Second Temple Judaism*. Leiden: Brill, 2003.

Neudecker, Reinhard. "'And You Shall Love Your Neighbor as Yourself—I Am the Lord' (Lev 19.18) in Jewish Interpretation." *Biblica* 73, no. 4 (1992): 496–517.

Osiek, Carolyn. "Female Slaves, *Porneia*, and the Limits of Obedience." In *Early Christian Families in Context: An Interdisciplinary Dialogue*, 255–76. Grand Rapids: Eerdmans, 2003.

Outler, Albert C., ed. *The Works of John Wesley*. Vol. 3. Nashville: Abingdon, 1986.

———, ed. *The Works of John Wesley*. Vol. 4. Nashville: Abingdon, 1987.

Parker, Angela N. *If God Still Breathes, Why Can't I? Black Lives Matter and Biblical Authority*. Grand Rapids: Eerdmans, 2021.

Perkins, Pheme. *Love Commands in the New Testament*. New York: Paulist Press, 1982.

Perry, Samuel L. "The Bible as a Product of Cultural Power: The Case of Gender Ideology in the English Standard Version." *Sociology of Religion* 81, no. 1 (2019): 68–92.

Piper, John, and Wayne Grudem, eds. *Recovering Biblical Manhood and Womanhood: A Response to Evangelical Feminism*. Wheaton: Crossway, 1991.

Preato, Dennis J. "Junia, A Female Apostle: An Examination of the Historical Record." *Priscilla Papers* 33, no. 2 (2019): 8–15.

Reinmuth, Titus. "Nehemiah 8 and the Authority of Torah in Ezra-Nehemiah." In *Unity and Disunity in Ezra-Nehemiah*, 241–62. Hebrew Bible Monographs 17. Sheffield: Sheffield Phoenix, 2008.

Rotelle, John E., ed. *Teaching Christianity: De Doctrina Christiana*. Translated by Edmund Hill. New York: New City Press, 1996.

Sandt, Huub van de, and Jurgen K. Zangenberg, eds. *Matthew, James, and Didache: Three Related Documents in Their Jewish and Christian Settings*. Symposium Series. Atlanta: SBL Press, 2008.

Schaff, Philip, ed. *The Nicene and Post-Nicene Fathers of the Christian Church*. Series 1. 14 vols. Grand Rapids: Eerdmans, 1994.

Schniedewind, William M. "The Chronicler as Interpreter of Scripture." In *The Chronicler as Author: Studies in Text and Texture*, 158–80. JSOT 263. Sheffield: Sheffield Academic Press, 1999.

Schnittjer, Gary Edward. *Old Testament Use of Old Testament: A Book by Book Guide*. Grand Rapids: Zondervan, 2021.

Segovia, Fernando F., and Mary Ann Tolbert, eds. *Reading from This Place*. Vol. 1, *Social Location and Biblical Interpretation in the United States*. Minneapolis: Fortress, 1995.

Sievers, Joseph, and Amy-Jill Levine, eds. *The Pharisees*. Grand Rapids: Eerdmans, 2021.

Skinner, Christopher. "Love One Another: The Johannine Love Command in the Farewell Discourse." In *Johannine Ethics: The Moral World of the Gospel and Epistles of John*, 25–42. Minneapolis: Fortress, 2017.

Stackert, Jeffrey. *Rewriting the Torah: Literary Revision in Deuteronomy and the Holiness Legislation*. Forschungen zum Alten Testament 52. Tübingen: Mohr Siebeck, 2007.

Thiessen, Matthew. *Jesus and the Forces of Death*. Grand Rapids: Baker, 2020.

Thompson, Geoff. "Metaphors for Scripture: Taking up Dale Martin's Challenge." *Theology* 123, no. 6 (2020): 405–13.

Trebilcock, Michelle R. "Towards a Theological Hermeneutic for Contexts of Change: Love in Liminality." PhD dissertation, Charles Sturt University, 2015.

Vatican II Council. "Dei Verbum: Dogmatic Constitution on Divine Revelation." http://www.vatican.va/archive/hist_coun cils/ii_vatican_council/documents/vat-ii_const_19651118_dei -verbum_en.html.

Venema, G. J. *Reading Scripture in the Old Testament*. Leiden: Brill, 2004.

Warner, Megan. "Therefore a Man Leaves His Father and His Mother and Clings to His Wife: Marriage and Intermarriage in Genesis 2:24." *Journal of Biblical Literature* 136, no. 2 (2017): 269–88.

Watson, Francis, and Sarah Parkhouse, eds. *Telling the Christian Story Differently*. London: T&T Clark, 2020.

Webster, John. *Word and Church: Essays in Christian Dogmatics*. Edinburgh: T&T Clark, 2001.

Wesley, John. *Sermons on Several Occasions*. London: Wesleyan Conference Office, 1872.

West, Gerald O. "Recovering the Biblical Story of Tamar: Training for Transformation, Doing Development." In *For Better for*

Worse: The Role of Religion in Development Cooperation, 135–206. Halmstad: Swedish Mission Council, 2016.

Whitters, Mark F. "The Persianized Liturgy of Nehemiah 8:1–8." *Journal of Biblical Literature* 136, no. 1 (2017): 63–84.

Wingren, Gustaf. *Luther on Vocation.* Translated by Carl C. Rasmussen. Eugene, OR: Wipf and Stock, n.d.

Wit, Hans de, and Gerald O. West, eds. *African and European Readers of the Bible in Dialogue: In Quest of a Shared Meaning.* Leiden: Brill, 2008.

Wollenberg, Rebecca Scharbach. "The Book That Changed: Narratives of Ezran Authorship as Late Antique Biblical Criticism." *Journal of Biblical Literature* 138, no. 1 (2019): 143–60.

Wood, A. Skevington. *The Principles of Biblical Interpretation: As Enunciated by Irenaeus, Origen, Augustine, Luther and Calvin.* Grand Rapids: Zondervan, 1967.

Work, Telford. *Living and Active: Scripture in the Economy of Salvation.* Grand Rapids: Eerdmans, 2002.

Wynkoop, Mildred Bangs. *A Theology of Love: The Dynamic of Wesleyanism.* 2nd ed. Kansas City: Beacon Hill Press, 2015.

Yoo, Philip Y. "On Nehemiah 8,8a." *Zeitschrift für die Alttestamentliche Wissenschaft* 127, no. 3 (2015): 502–7. https://doi.org/10.1515/zaw-2015-0029.

Young, Frances. *Ways of Reading Scripture: Collected Papers.* Wissenschaftliche Untersuchungen zum Neuen Testament 369. Tübingen: Mohr Siebeck, 2018.

Zahn, Molly M. *Rethinking Rewritten Scripture: Composition and Exegesis in the 4QReworked Pentateuch Manuscripts.* Studies on the Texts of the Desert of Judah 95. Leiden: Brill, 2011.

Ziegler, Philip G. "On the Present Possibility of Sola Scriptura." *International Journal of Systematic Theology* (2022): 1–19.

Scripture Index